WILD
BLUEBERRIES

To Mr. Smooth ~
 What a fine and
special man you are...
Smart, funny, perceptive,
kind, unpretentious, generous,
deeply wise ~ and calm as
a Northern lake at daybreak.
It's been a pleasure knowing you
 all these years, though regrettably
we've seen each other far too seldom.
     Be well and hugs to you, Peter

WILD BLUEBERRIES

Tales of Nuns, Rabbits & Discovery in Rural Michigan

Peter Damm

O'BRIEN & WHITAKER
EASTSOUND, WASHINGTON
2019

Copyright © 2019 by Peter L. Damm
All rights reserved.

First Edition
ISBN 978-0-9668431-3-2

O'Brien & Whitaker Publishers
Eastsound, Washington 98245
info@bokubooks.com

Design by Marian O'Brien
Illustrations by Suzanne Anderson-Carey
Author Photograph by Meoy Gee
Available in print and e-book format.

No part of this book may be reproduced in any form or by an electronic or mechanical means, including information storage and retrieval systems, without written permission from the author, except for the use of brief quotations in a book review.

In respect for the privacy of various people, some names and/or identifying characteristics have been changed.

To Bess and Big John
who have slipped beyond the boundaries
of this physical world

and

To the memory of Leo Litwak ~ gifted writer, teacher,
philosopher, courageous medic in WWII ~ one of the
finest human beings I have ever had the privilege and
pleasure to know. Leo passed away July 27, 2018 and on
that date each coming year I shall raise a toast high to
honor this unique and very special man.
Goodbye Leo. We miss you.

Part I
Rosetta Stones

Rabbits	15
Roll Call	19
Father	25
Superstition	31
Baseball	33
St. Michael & the Blessed Virgin	36
Susan	40
Mother	44
Snowballs	56
Hell	64
Animal Crackers	68
Fishing	74
Holy Orders	87
Tigers	94
Putsy	103

THE LITTLE ONES	120
SIN	123
TRIBES	131
WILD BLUEBERRIES	138
HOLY COMMUNION	146
THE KNOTHOLE	153
PLAYING	160
DREAMING	166
ANCESTORS	171
LEAVING	179

PART II
MOONRISE

WEATHER	187
FATHER	195

"If I attempt to distinguish between fiction and memory, and press my nose to memory's glass to see more clearly, the remembered image grows more illusive, like the details of a Pointillist painting. I recognize it, more than I see it. This recognition is a fabric of emotion as immaterial as music. In this defect of memory do we have the emergence of imagination?... Precisely where memory is frail and emotion is strong, imagination takes fire."

WRIGHT MORRIS
"EARTHLY DELIGHTS, UNEARTHLY ADORNMENTS"

PART I
ROSETTA STONES

Rabbits

I come from a large family, by modern standards at least. Six kids—five boys and a girl. Nine of us altogether, counting my parents and Winky, our dog. Winky was part Collie, part Irish Setter or Golden Retriever and as much one of the family as any of us. Our family would have gotten bigger. My mother had three miscarriages, two after I was born. I'm the youngest of the six who made it. When people found out how many kids were in my family, they always said: "Catholics, eh?" Nobody had as many kids as Catholics.

    I remember reading a newspaper story about Sonny Liston, the heavyweight boxing champion of the world. He would soon be laid flat by the then Cassius Clay with a phantom six-inch punch nobody saw. The story said that Sonny was the 24th of 25 children. "Now that's a big family," I said to myself, thrilled that my own seemed small by comparison.

"Those Catholics are just like rabbits," I heard people whisper. At first I didn't understand what they meant. But later I realized they were talking about having babies. Rabbits had lots of babies and so did Catholics. But I couldn't understand why rabbits and Catholics, in particular, had so many babies and why Methodists, for instance, or Presbyterians, did not. Or nuns. It was the nuns who baffled me most. They were women and Catholics, yet they never had babies. When I was in Catholic grade school I tried endlessly to solve this riddle. I even applied my version of Aristotelian logic to the problem. The syllogism went something like this:

> Women have babies;
> Catholic women have lots of babies;
> Nuns are both Catholic and women
>   (and holier than the rest, and babies are
>   a blessing from God)
> Therefore, nuns should have lots and lots of babies.

But they didn't. Figure that out.

I played a little poker as a kid. Let's be truthful. I played a lot of poker as a kid. So I had some grasp of chance and mathematical probabilities. I spent hours trying to figure the odds that, given any random group of women, including nuns, only the nuns would never get pregnant. The odds seemed impossible to me, like drawing an inside royal flush a hundred times out of a hundred. I'd never had a single royal flush in my whole life. The probability had to run in the millions.

Something else must be at work here, I decided. But what? Perhaps it was supernatural. Maybe God and the nuns had made a deal that they simply wouldn't get pregnant. This was in His power to do. He had decided, after all, to make the trees green and the sky blue. He could have made them purple and chartreuse instead. He told the Angel of Death to pass over the Jews' houses in the Old Testament. He could also order the stork to pass the nuns by. That way, women who didn't like children could become nuns. It was a perfect arrangement. This explained a lot about the way the nuns treated us at school.

I finally decided that the key to the mystery lay in the layers of long robes and habits that the nuns always wore. They actually got pregnant—we just couldn't tell. The nuns weren't called penguins for nothing. They wore floor-length black robes with starched, pure white collars that were a foot long and looked like chest protectors. On their heads they wore long black habits that flowed down like capes.

They could be pregnant with triplets and no one would ever know, I thought. I started watching. I looked for signs of expanding bellies beneath the black robes. A few times I was sure that I'd discovered a pregnant nun, one who looked plumper and plumper. But in the end I could never be certain. Just when I thought the evidence was getting really conclusive, we'd go on summer vacation. By autumn the particular nun would be transferred to another school (so we were told) or not look as large as I remembered (which meant she'd had the baby over the summer).

I always wondered what happened to these babies the nuns had. Finally I figured it out. They must quietly give them to Catholic families all over the diocese. That would explain why the Catholics had so many children in comparison to the Methodists and Presbyterians. Those religions didn't have nuns who were constantly adding to the number of babies being born. Maybe there were some of these "nun-babies" in my own family. Two of my brothers were redheads and didn't look anything like the rest of us. But that was alright. We were all Children of God and Steve (he and Mike were the redheads) built model airplanes and ships that I loved. But every now and then, when he had one of his redheaded temper tantrums, I wished the nuns had given him to someone else.

Roll Call

I grew up in a small town: Flushing, Michigan. When I met kids from other places during the summertime, I was always embarrassed. They would ask me where I lived. I would say Flushing and could tell by their smirks that it made them think of toilets.

When I was twelve we moved to another town thirty miles away, but this didn't help much. The town was named Grand Blanc—pronounced "Grand Blank" in Anglicized Michiganese. But I had to admit that there was a certain pathetic accuracy in the description, an instance of life imitating phonetics. Grand Blanc was "The Big White" to the French trappers who named it, but to those of us growing up there it was simply "Grand Blank," the Big Zero. I was afraid the name would taint me, that I would become a grand blank as well. "Why can't we live in a town named Moccasin Flat, or Grand Heritage, or View from the Top of the Mountain?" I wondered. Something that sparked the imagination in a more uplifting, lyrical way than Flushing or Grand Blanc.

I have always been sensitive about names. If you'd grown up with a last name like "Damm" you'd be sensitive too. I hated my name. I felt like I bore a scarlet nameplate on my chest. It spawned dozens of jokes, repeated hundreds of times. "Damn, nice to meet you." "Hot damn!" "How's the whole Damn family?" These were always followed by guffaws of laughter. Everyone thought their joke was the first.

Having a name like Damm and also being Catholic creates certain...complications. These were amplified by the 1950's. If you've forgotten the Fifties or were not yet born, it was a time of staid moral conservatism. Dwight David Eisenhower was president. The Cold War iced its way across the political landscape. Joe McCarthy kept America fixed upon the Communist scourge, and a single gyrating pelvis (male and fully clothed, no less) scandalized the nation. When Elvis finally performed on The Ed Sullivan Show the camera showed him only from the waist up. Swearing was not condoned. "Four-letter words" were never heard on television or seen in print. For a Catholic, swearing was a sin, and my name was a four-letter word.

I vividly remember my first day in sixth grade. My family had moved that summer from Flushing to Grand Blanc. We now lived in an old farmhouse four miles out of town and three-quarters of a mile down a dirt road. We had few neighbors and it was difficult to get to town. As a result my brother Steve and I (we were the two youngest and couldn't drive) didn't get to know many kids. We shagged a

Roll Call

lot of fly balls in the backyard that summer. In the fall Steve would enter the ninth grade at the public high school and I would go to Holy Family, the Catholic grade school.

I felt strange and apprehensive long before I arrived at Holy Family that first day. I'd never worn a uniform. Navy blue trousers, light blue shirts, and a little red tie. The tie criss-crossed below the collar to form an upside-down "V" with a snap in the middle of the criss-cross. I felt like a Martian corporal.

My father dropped me off at school that day. After he drove away I stood on the sidewalk for a good ten minutes. I didn't want to be here. I wanted to be back in Flushing, despite its name. All my friends were there. My life was there.

I glanced around and saw uniforms everywhere. Dark blue, light blue, and little red ties. Even the girls wore dark blue skirts, white blouses and little ties. It was like being surrounded by funhouse mirrors; everywhere I looked I saw my own image, only the shapes were distorted and the sizes different.

Kids talked and laughed in groups. A few of us hung tentative and alone on the periphery. A loud bell rang. The mass of blue uniforms slowly split and moved towards separate doorways, like a school of fish dividing. Signs were taped to the classroom doors inside: 3rd Grade; 5th Grade; 8th Grade. I found an empty seat toward the back of the sixth grade room and sat down. A nun dressed in her long black penguin robes and starched white collar stood beside the door.

After a few minutes the nun walked to her desk and the commotion settled down. She introduced herself as Sister

Michael. This struck a sudden chord in me. Maybe that was the reason nuns didn't have babies. Most of them had men's names. Sister William. Sister Joseph. Sister Bruno. The principal at St. Robert's in Flushing was Sister Angelica, but she didn't match the image that her name conjured up. She was a battle-axe, 6'1" tall, pock-marked, powerful, and mean. She reminded me of Bronko Nagurski, the mighty fullback/defensive tackle for the Chicago Bears.

Sister Michael looked young, feminine and rather shy. Her skin was smooth and very white. She started reading the roll and I got nervous. I'd been dreading this moment—the reading of my name—for weeks.

"Diane Adams," she began.

"Here."

"David Banks."

Silence.

"David Banks?" she repeated, looking up.

"He's got a cold," someone called out.

Sister Michael bent low over her roll book and made a mark in it.

"Monica Carson," she continued.

"Here."

She was getting closer. My breath got short and my palms started sweating.

"Karen Dailey."

"Here."

"Peter...."

She stopped. I looked up in terror to see her face turning red. The class's attention suddenly focused like a bird dog catching the scent of a pheasant. Something was

Roll Call

up. Some new kid's name was impossible to pronounce, some nine-syllabled Polish tongue-twister that would be perfect for a little good old fashioned ridicule.

"Peter D..." She couldn't get it out. C'mon, lady, just say it. Say it!

"Peter D... D... DAMM!" she blurted out.

She couldn't have made it worse if she had set off firecrackers. She'd probably never said the word in her life. The class broke up. "Damn!" someone yelled from the back with a mock southern twang. Everyone looked around to see what poor slob would own up to such a name.

I shrank to the size of a toadstool. I tried to disappear. I wanted to strangle this nun (certainly a sinful thought).

"H — —" My voice cracked. Everyone's head spun around to look at me. "Here!" I said loudly, with an edge of defiance. A kid in the back made a remark. The class laughed and I stared right at him until an uneasy silence fell on the room. It was 8:10 in the morning and I already hated this place.

Over the next few weeks a strange thing happened. I made a lot of friends. I was accepted more quickly than the other new kids. I realized in retrospect that this happened because of my name. After that first roll call everyone knew me. It was my rite of passage into the group.

I even became a bridge to the forbidden. I made swearing legal. What had previously been a sin was now just a name. "Damn" and "Damn it!" flew around the playground like autumn leaves in a windstorm. Some kid would be pulled off the playground by his ear, accused of saying the "D-word."

"But, Sister, we were playing tag and Pete was it. I just yelled 'Damm's it!' so everyone would know. I didn't do anything wrong. It's his name, Sister." Grudgingly she would let him go. He'd come back with a sly grin. This drove the nuns crazy. They were like tax collectors who knew they were being cheated but couldn't figure out how to stop it. But sometimes even the nuns joined in. When innocent Sister Michael became particularly exasperated with me she would shout a loud "Mister DAMM!" and I could sense a small spasm of pleasure as she uttered the forbidden word.

Father

I was the youngest and also the smallest. I was no match for my brothers' strength. I got cuffed around in family fights. So did my sister, Susan. Species adapt to promote their survival, and my sister and I did the same. Strength was not our long suit so we became quick-witted, agile and fast. We were like foxes. I was hell in a game of tag because no one could catch me, and Susan was even faster. I was fifteen before I could beat her in a footrace.

To go with my speed I became a chameleon. It was a defense mechanism. My colors could change like a snowshoe rabbit's in winter. Instead of developing my own identity, I took on the coloring of those around me. I could fit in like a green bug on a leaf. I felt safer that way, less threatened.

But Susan and I were also battlers. We would run only so far before we turned to fight. Then we were very tough, like deer who battle head-on with their antlers until they drop. We got this from our father. His main character trait was strength, not speed. He was powerful. He never ran in his life except for public office, to become City Attorney of Flint or Attorney General of the State of Michigan on the Democratic ticket in 1952. He narrowly lost in a year when Eisenhower trounced Adlai Stevenson and the Republicans routed the Democrats at nearly every level of Michigan politics.

John Damm. Johnny Damm in the years before his eldest son was born. Then he became Big John and his son was Johnny. Integrity and strength were his hallmarks. Flint was a car town: Buick, Chevrolet, Fisher Body, AC Sparkplug. Little Detroit. Big John labored at the vortex of the sometimes corrupt political and union machinery, but

FATHER

you couldn't buy him off or flatter him into deals.

"They can take everything from you, one way or another," he said to us, "but they can never take your integrity. Only you can give that away." It was his chief lesson to me. He was a lawyer who dealt with contracts, technicalities and signatures all his life, but his own signature was never necessary. When he gave his word, he kept it. It was as straightforward and simple as that.

Johnny Damm was born in Cleveland in 1910. As a kid he delivered nickel buckets of beer and boxed rounds at his dad's theatre as entertainment between shows. His father successively owned three independent theatres in Cleveland and Wadsworth, Ohio before he was forced out of business by the big chains.

Grandpa booked a variety of entertainment. Some movies. Vaudeville. Many of the great Negro acts of the day. This was the late 20's and prosperity reigned.

The '29 crash came early in my dad's college years. Johnny Damm lettered in football, baseball and debate at Heidelberg College in Tiffin, won the intramural tennis doubles championship, was captain of the baseball team and one of the leading hitters in the state of Ohio. He repaired tracks for the Erie Railroad in the summer—ten hours a day, six days a week, for 35 cents an hour. It was hard, physical labor in the hot sun, then he played baseball after work. He was a hard-hitting first baseman. "I always loved batting with men on base and the game on the line. I figured it was the pitcher who was in trouble because he had to get the ball past me," he told me. Those words always haunted me as I stood at the plate late in a close game, terrified that I'd strike out with Dad in the stands. He played semi-pro level baseball, but he'd torn up his right knee playing football in high school and it slowed him just enough to make the Big Leagues a step out of reach. The musculature of that right leg remained smaller than the left his whole life. Medicine wasn't so sophisticated in the 1920's. There were no arthroscopic miracles that had you back on the field ten days later. Surgical instruments were steak knives by comparison with ours.

His last year at Heidelberg the college dean called him into his office.

"I was wondering if you know what work you will pursue after graduation, Mr. Damm."

"No, sir. I don't really know what I'll do. I've thought about working with my father, but I'm not sure I want to do that."

Dean Kennedy looked at the young man in front of him for a few moments.

"Have you ever considered studying the law?" he asked.

There was a pause.

"Well, no sir, I haven't."

"Perhaps you should give it some thought. I think you would make an excellent attorney. I would be happy to write letters of recommendation for you."

This was an utterly new idea and it took root in him. The next fall he entered the University of Michigan Law School in Ann Arbor. The whole direction of his life changed because of one ten-minute conversation and one man's interest.

Johnny Damm honed his strength, integrity and determination in those years. He went to law school in the depth of the Depression, 1932-35, working for his meals by washing dishes in the Law Club and spending summers on the railroad. He won the prestigious Case Club Competition, arguing a mock trial before justices of the Michigan Supreme Court and a Federal judge, and was elected president of the Law Club.

After graduating he returned to Tiffin to marry my mother, whom he had met at Heidelberg. They moved to Mt. Pleasant, Michigan, where he started a law practice and worked as a wildcatter on the oil rigs at night to make ends meet. Two sons, Johnny and Mike, were born.

It wasn't always easy growing up as the child of a rough-hewn, four-sport, law-club-president wildcatter molded on the guts and sacrifice of the Depression who was as honest as a forest oak and just about as strong. And who felt the pressure of raising six not-exactly-retiring offspring amidst campaigns, elections, labor strikes, trials, diabetes and too-frequent trips to the bottle.

But if we battled and there were years when I hated his guts, he taught me more than I know and gave me a set of principles that are my keel in the world.

"They can take everything from you, one way or another, but they can never take your integrity. Only you can give that away."

Superstition

Some people are born superstitious. I was not. I became that way with time. My birthday was the cause. I was born on January 13th. Not only was it the thirteenth day of the month, it was also Friday the 13th, that unluckiest of days. My young mind built an intriguing construction from this confluence of facts. I became increasingly superstitious, but turned the normal signs of bad luck into signals of charm and good fortune. I regularly walked under ladders. I broke mirrors now and again for good luck, and developed first an affection, then a passion, for black cats. If I saw one down the street I'd change course to make certain it crossed my path.

Thirteen became my magic number. I considered it a talisman. Players on sports teams never wear the number thirteen (except for pitcher Ralph Branca, who was wearing thirteen when he served up the most famous home run in baseball history, Bobby Thomson's ninth-inning "shot heard 'round the world." It broke the hearts of the Brooklyn Dodgers and sent the New York Giants to the World Series against the Yankees in 1951). Athletes think thirteen is unlucky. I thought differently. Once it took me two weeks to convince my baseball coach to let me wear thirteen on my jersey. I batted .428 that year. My football coach never relented and I had to wear number forty-two (maybe that's why I dropped that touchdown pass against Clio). I loved all Fridays the 13th. The only day I loved more than my birthday was that rare occasion when the original double re-converged—when my birthday fell on Friday the 13th.

In my contrary system of superstitions all the normal good luck charms still held their magic. No inverse force was created. Four-leaf clovers, rabbits' feet, spilling salt—all of them were good luck to me.

The Catholic Church doesn't smile on such superstitious notions. Especially if you're older than seven, "the Age of Reason" (why we suddenly possess reason at age seven I could never figure out). The Church views superstitions as worse than poppycock. They cross into the realm of sin. Realizing this fact and being semi-reasonable, I didn't tell the priest about my superstitions. I kept them to myself. I figured that since I'd had the splendid ill fortune to be born on Friday the 13th, I had a special dispensation.

Baseball

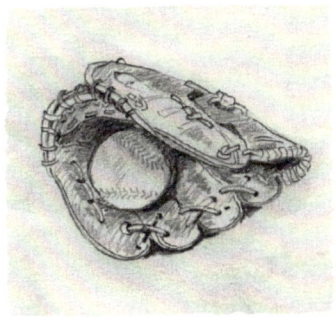

Our ball fields didn't have fences. They were bordered by "the weeds," that region beyond the mowed or tromped down outfield where order ended and frustration began. We lost countless balls in the weeds, with both teams stomping down the long grass and thistles, trying to feel the ball underfoot, because if we didn't find it, the game was over.

    My brother, Steve, was a vexation in these games. He was bigger than everyone else, hefty, coordinated and strong. He hit towering home runs that made even his teammates groan—they required another long tromp in the weeds. A skill required to play the outfield (in addition to good defense and an arm) was the ability to "spot," to locate balls in the long grass. You couldn't take your eyes off the ball for a split second. You had to watch it land and run straight to the spot, single-mindedly, like a Labrador retriever going after a duck. If you didn't find the ball right away, you threw your glove down to mark where you thought the ball landed so the search didn't drift too far afield. Years later I wondered how many of our old baseballs the bulldozers plowed under as they cleared another field for a subdivision.

Steve was both a blessing and a curse. In addition to his prowess at the plate, he was the best pitcher. He had a searing fastball and was just wild enough to make batters edgy. If you get hit by a hard fastball, it hurts—a lot. So when we chose up sides everyone wanted to be on Steve's team. And those home runs he hit were flights of awe and beauty. But they always meant another twenty minutes stomping the weeds.

There was one field in town where playing with Steve was simply a blessing—Little League at Flushing Park. He would hit those titanic home runs, past the outfielders, over the park road, the lawn beyond, and into the Flint River. No one else ever did that. Such feats seemed beyond the laws of nature. People would gather and watch the ball bob and float away on the current. But it was okay because the umpire always had more balls. The game didn't end and we didn't have to go searching.

I was a center fielder. I nearly wrote, "I played center field." But that doesn't reflect the strength of the self image. It's not full or round enough. At the age of ten or twelve I thought of myself as a center fielder in the way people think of themselves as Jewish, Catholic, Norwegian or as composers. It was a part of my identity. It reflected my place in the world. Center field was my territory, my domain. I never played shortstop or third base or left field. Center field existed and I was a center fielder.

This identity developed over time. Baseball was in my blood, passed from my father to my brothers and me. In the summertime, from about the age of three onward, a baseball glove accompanied me like a third hand. Hit a ball in the air and I'd catch it. I didn't have a great throwing arm. I wasn't great with ground balls. But I was faster than everyone else. I could run down fly balls no one else could get close to, and if I got there I could catch almost anything. There was grace and exhilaration in these headlong dashes over the green pastures of the outfield. It was like being a hawk with a great blue sky to soar in. I used to pray that the batter would hit a long drive deep into the alley. I would race over, dive or leap up high, snatching the ball from its flight. There was ego in this impulse, and desire. Showing off. But also a pure love of the movement and grace. This was my passion, my art. I loved to leap and snag a high fly ball the way a Barishnikov loved to leap in "Giselle." I could shag fly balls for hours on end. It was my ecstasy, my perfect place in the world.

ST. MICHAEL & THE BLESSED VIRGIN

"In nomine Patris, et Filii, et Spiritus Sancti. Amen."
"In the name of the Father, and of the Son, and of the Holy Ghost."

Times have changed. The third figure of the Trinity isn't called the Holy Ghost anymore. Now he's called the "Holy Spirit." Spiritus Sancti. But when I was growing up He was the Holy Ghost, the Big Spook.

I never knew what to make of this cryptic, rather sinister figure. I could picture God the Father. He was imposing, stern, even fearsome—my father with a long white beard. Christ was more beneficent and human. He healed the sick. He died for our sins on the Cross. He cried in His pain and brokenness atop Golgotha: "Father. Father. Why hast thou forsaken me?" He had long brown hair, a beard, and prominent, well-defined calf muscles (I always envied His calves because mine were so skinny).

But what to make of this "Holy Ghost"? He was mysterious, inscrutable, the spectre of the Godhead. His signature was a floating tongue of flame, like the Lone Ranger's was a silver bullet and Zorro's the letter Z cut with the point of his sword. Mystery defined them all. Disappearance. Cut and run. So I contemplated the Holy Ghost with a sense of both caution and allure. But ghosts do not conjure up comforting images in the minds of young children. I wasn't drawn toward the Holy Ghost for solace.

I inclined, instead, toward St. Michael the Archangel. He was my favorite, the Angel of Angels, with his sleek wings and white robes. He always hovered about three feet off the ground. I liked that. And he never had to move his wings. He could hover, fly through space, or instantaneously "appear" anywhere in the universe, all without moving his wings. The wings were for show, a mark of station, like the fins on a '58 Cadillac.

St. Michael was handsome, articulate and versatile, a blend of courage and refinement. He battled Lucifer, that evil genius, and cast him out of heaven. Later he announced the Immaculate Conception to the Blessed Virgin Mary. He appeared in her garden one day, hovered three feet off the ground, and announced to Mary that she'd been selected to be the Mother of God. She would, in fact, have the baby soon. Imagine Mary's surprise. God had, in effect, made love to her and she hadn't even gotten to enjoy it. Could God the Father have stolen some small orgasmic shudder from this act, under the guise that it was necessary if His Son were to be born to save mankind? Or did the fertilized egg which would be Christ just appear in Mary's womb the way St. Michael appeared in her garden, a kind of divine artificial insemination?

The announcement must have required some readjustment on Mary's part. What if she didn't want to be a mother just then, much less the Mother of God? Talk about performance anxiety.

But since God knows all, even in the future, He would have seen Mary's reactions before she had them. He would have picked the right person to be the Blessed Mother.

But why was Mary picked? I always wondered. The selection process intrigued me. Did God the Father, Son and Holy Ghost appoint a commission of high angels to search the files of the As Yet Unborn for the top five candidates? And what if the Trinity disagreed on the best choice? I would hope God the Son had the final word—she would be His Mother, after all. He had to live with her. But that would go against the patriarchy and God the Father isn't soft on such points, just as the Pope isn't soft on birth control.

Also, the final selection had to be made several generations before it was announced. Christ's mother had to be perfect and pure and free from sin. She would be the only human being since Adam and Eve were tossed out of the Garden of Paradise to be born without the blight of original sin on her soul. This required substantial pre-planning to fulfill the endless prophecies from Scripture foretelling the Messiah's coming. An entire wing of heaven, with thousands of angels, must have been dedicated to coordinating the thicket of interrelated events.

All this raised a question in my demented young mind: How did Mary's selection as God's Mother and her total freedom from sin fit with the Church's doctrine of free will? If it was determined beforehand that, by definition, she could never commit a sin, this certainly cut down her options for behavior. She couldn't disobey her parents, lie, swear, or smack her bratty cousin. She must have been an insufferable goody two shoes. How could she have had any friends? After such a childhood maybe she wasn't surprised when St. Michael floated into her garden and delivered his Mother of God/Immaculate Conception speech. It probably explained a lot.

At the age of eight or nine, the extraordinary nature of the Immaculate Conception was lost on me. I had no idea what "conception" was, immaculate or otherwise (I would have been spared considerable fretting about mathematical probabilities and the mystery of nuns not getting pregnant if I had). As I grew older and understood more about "conception" and the physical drives that fuel it, I decided that Joseph, Mary's husband, must have led a strange life. He slept in the same house, the same room (the same bed?) with this paragon of femininity, the perfect madonna— but he could never touch her. What did he do with his urges? Then there's the other question: what did Mary do with hers?

Susan

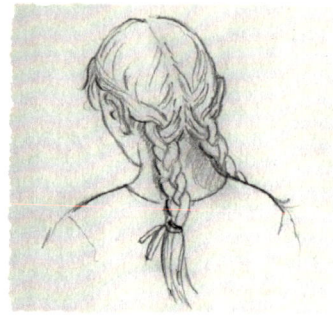

I both envied and pitied my sister, Susan. Being the only girl with five brothers has its equal portions of trial and privilege. She was at once madonna and demon, princess and pariah. We were boys. She was "a girl." We worshipped and disrespected her, challenged and protected her.

I liked Susan more than my brothers. She was gentler, not so filled with confrontation and aggression. But she was also a tomboy. She didn't have much choice. She was outnumbered. With five brothers always climbing trees, throwing balls and jumping fences, she developed certain characteristics as part of the tribe. She could do most anything we could, including take care of herself. She was tough, with wiry muscles. She and I had more than a few fights and I usually didn't fare well.

If Susan took on certain of our "male" traits, the influence also passed in the opposite direction. No male/

Susan

female division of labor existed among us children, due simply to the preponderance of boys. There was too much work to do. Our mother needed help. I grew up dusting furniture, sweeping floors, washing dishes and ironing clothes. Ironing was a special talent of mine. In the wintertime I loved the warmth of standing over the ironing board as the steam billowed up from damp sheets, shirts and pillow cases. I bankrolled milkshakes and a bow and arrow set from my ironing proceeds. The weekends were my big cash nights. Everyone rushed to get ready for this date or that basketball game, only to discover that the particular shirt, blouse or pair of pants they wanted was a wrinkled mess at the bottom of a clothes basket. For a quarter I would solve their problem. And I solved it well. I took pride in my ironing. For another quarter they could get their shoes shined, brown or black. Saddle shoes were a dime extra. Big families have certain advantages, such as their own internal economy.

I loved Susan's braids. They fell down her back like

intricate woven ropes and made her look like an Indian. She would sit on the bed in front of my mother and I watched in fascination as Mom braided her hair. She'd run a comb down the middle, take the hair on one side and divide it into three equal parts, then begin the delicate, fluid dance with her fingers and the strands of hair that somehow ended in long, perfect braids.

I loved this ritual and the graceful beauty of its movements. I could watch it day after day. Sometimes Mom even let me try, but I could never do it right. I'd get confused halfway through about which length of hair wound around where next, I'd pull them so tight that Susan would wince, or not weave the braids tightly enough. So my mother would finish and the braids ended up just right.

When Susan got older she had migraine headaches. I was twelve or thirteen. She would disappear into her room, sometimes for two or three days. The pain would be so bad in her head that she couldn't turn over. She couldn't move or get out of bed. Sometimes I sat a vigil outside her bedroom door. I could hear her moan and cry out and each time my stomach twisted that my sister was suffering so. It made me cry. I wanted desperately to know where such pain came from so I could take it away. But I found no answers, and the mystery of it frightened me. When I brought things in to her she would be lying on her side, pulled up in a ball. A shirt or pillow covered her eyes to keep the light out and her hands pressed against her skull as if to keep it from bursting. I would think of Christ on the Cross, crying out in his agony.

Susan

Susan must have felt as forsaken and alone, isolated in the solitary chamber of her pain.

A few days later she would emerge from her room, her face drawn and her eyes dark. She felt better and was relieved that the ordeal was over. But I could see the fear living inside of her, the fear of when the pain would swoop down with no warning and ravage her again.

Mother

My mother grew up in Tiffin, Ohio, the oldest of four girls with no brothers. It struck me as a curious generational counterbalance that she would give birth to five sons.

Tiffin had three claims to moderate fame in my mind. First, my cousins lived there. This was important because we sometimes went to visit them. Secondly, it was the site of Heidelberg College, where both my parents went to school and met. But most importantly, Tiffin was the home of Ballreich's Potato Chips. Every Christmas my Great Uncle George shipped us a big gold tin, two feet high, full of Ballreich's. I was a potato chip lover and Ballreich's were the tastiest chips I'd ever eaten. They were salty and rippled and lots of them curled over double. Just before Christmas I'd run home from school every day to see if the tin from Uncle George had come yet. When it finally arrived I pried off the lid, sat down on the floor with the big tin nestled between my legs, and ate most of my share on the spot. I stuffed the crisp chips in my mouth with abandon, the way a man lost in the desert drinks water.

A lot of Catholics lived in Tiffin when my mother was growing up. There were two parishes, one on each side of town. In a neat bit of theological symmetry, one was named St. Mary's and the other St. Joseph's. My mother's family attended St. Joseph's and she went to Catholic grade school.

When Mom was eleven years old her father got sick with a flu and fever. It turned into pneumonia and inside of a week he was dead. He was not a sickly man. This was 1924, before the discovery of penicillin. He was forty-one years old and strong, a printer. He and one of his five brothers had started Sullivan Printing. When Mom was walking home from school that day she saw Father Hultgen, the parish priest, walking a little in front of her on the sidewalk. He was carrying the Blessed Sacrament and didn't speak with anyone. For three or four blocks they walked on in distant tandem, the priest in front, the little girl a ways behind. Then, startlingly, the priest turned up the walk to her house. She stopped in confusion and alarm as he walked up the steps and entered the front door. She ran up the walk after him. Once inside, she was hurried upstairs to her parents' bedroom.

Most of the family was in the room. A nurse and Dr. Magers, their family doctor and old friend, were there. Aunt Cora and Aunt Lula, her father's only two sisters to survive childhood, knelt near the bed next to her mother, who was crying. Father Hultgen placed his purple stole for administering the sacraments around his neck. He prayed over her father, anointed his forehead and said the Last Rites. Twenty minutes later Mom's father was dead.

His body remained in the house, as was the custom in those days. He was laid out in the casket at one end of the living room, in front of the fireplace. People came by to pay their respects.

The family went into shock. Mom's mother, who was dead by the time I was born, "never completely recovered." She was thirty-nine years old with four daughters—ages two, six, eight and eleven—and suddenly a widow.

My mother is most comfortable when she's taking care of someone. She was the oldest daughter and learned the role early. Then she raised six kids of her own and nursed her husband through diabetes, bouts of alcoholism, prostate cancer and bone cancer. Self-sacrifice is her ethic, her way of being in the world.

I remember Aunt Cora and Uncle George. I was very little when they were in their eighties and nineties. Aunt Cora was a small, gnarled old lady. She was warm, prayed a lot, and laughed. She gave me old coins wrapped in cloth—ancient pennies, dimes, and Indian head nickels. I can still picture Uncle George. He could barely walk and was nearly deaf. We had to yell to make him hear us. He sat for hours in a deep, stuffed chair, his bony arms atop the high armrests like a heron's wings just before it flies. I was a little afraid of him because he was old and we had to yell at him. But I loved him because he was like a second father to my mother and had sent us Ballreich's Potato Chips every Christmas of my life.

MOTHER

My mother's handwriting was illegible. Especially to an eight-year-old. Many days after school she would send me to the A & P or King's Butcher Shop. They were both on Main Street, in the two blocks of stores that made up downtown Flushing. There was a Western Auto, where we got flashlight batteries, baseballs and the model airplanes that my brother, Steve, labored over compulsively; Luce's Pharmacy where we drank Cherry Cokes at the soda fountain; a four-lane bowling alley at the end of the block; and Rupe's Barber Shop. Rupe was the barber's first name. He was there long before I was born.

King's was next to the pharmacy, two steps up from the sidewalk. The butchers were always impeccable. They wore white coats, starched and pressed.

"What can I get for you today, Petie?" Mr. King would say from behind the counter, his coat bright white and his hair neatly combed and parted.

I would look down at the list my mother had written, trying to make it out.

"Uh...three pounds of...ground...ground beef. Two... two..." I would reply haltingly. Then Mr. King and I would set about trying to decipher the list. It was a ritual between us. Her handwriting was like the scrawls and squiggles of a minimalist painter — meaning was present there somewhere, but we had to struggle hard to discern it. Some minutes later, our decoding accomplished, Mr. King would weigh out my purchases, wrap them neatly in sheets of white paper off a roll on the wall, and secure the paper with a large red rubber band.

I have never seen these big rubber bands anywhere else. I loved them. They were maybe eight inches long. I would hook one end over the tip of my left thumb, straighten my arm out in front of me, then pull back the other end to my ear with my right hand, like drawing a bow. The rubber bands were powerful, accurate and silent. I shot them like arrows, playing endless games of stealth and cunning. I'd be an Indian scout in the upstairs hallway, shooting through the open bedroom door at the knobs on dresser drawers. In the summertime I'd practice outside. My aim got so good that I could whirl around 180 degrees while pulling back my rubber band and shoot the top off a dandelion at twenty feet, all in one motion.

The problem with my mother's handwriting began when she was in high school. She took typing and shorthand and was good enough to compete in a statewide competition. The shorthand was the culprit. I contend it eroded her physical ability to form the 26 letters of the Roman alphabet.

Mother

This skill may have helped pay her way through college but it caused endless confusion to her offspring, the butcher, and the clerks at the A & P.

My whole life, whenever she'd send me a letter, it took me into the second day to figure out what she'd written, to decipher the meaning. I think of her letters as tiny Rosetta Stones, like I think of the events in my life.

My mother washed a lot of clothes. Six kids, five boys. The "Damn Boys" people called us in Flushing, though not entirely with malice. We weren't bad kids, just active, into everything. We'd keep a pair of blue jeans clean about four minutes. We took pride in our ability to get really dirty. It was a measure of manliness at the tender age of six or seven.

I remember my mother hanging clothes on the line. Wherever we lived, day after day, she hung clothes on the line. Three loads a day was normal. In the days before automatic washers and dryers three loads was a lot of laundry, a lot of washing-rinsing-wringing-hanging-drying-folding-ironing-putting away of laundry. It was a lot of clothespins. We had a bushel basket just for clothespins. I considered clothespins one of mankind's simple but brilliant inventions. What would we have done each afternoon without them?

Basements were necessary in the Midwest back then. Basements weren't just a place to store old books, sleds, and warped badminton rackets. They were where you hung your clothes to dry when it rained or during the long, cold winters. Our basement was criss-crossed with clotheslines, five or six inches apart, strung back and forth in smooth arcs like telephone wires, just below the wooden beams.

When Mom hung up clothes she wore a cloth apron around her waist with pouches in front for the clothespins, like a carpenter wears for his nails. She would move back and forth along the lines with a graceful deftness, wasting no space or pins. She would hang up nine shirts by their tails and use only ten clothespins. She'd hang the sheets on the back line, closest to the wall. The towels went in front of them, then the pants, the shirts, the T-shirts, dish towels, and finally the underpants, hankies and socks. These didn't hang down so far so it was easier to get to the longer clothes hanging further back.

Spring and summer were my mother's favorite seasons. She loved her peonies and irises and the freshness of the clothes when they dried in the air and sunshine. She was able to spend more time outdoors. Often when the clothes were hanging outside, nearly dry, a sudden rain storm would sweep across the land. We'd all scramble into the backyard, like children running out of school in a firedrill, to pull the clothes off the clotheslines. We'd fling towels and pillow cases over our arms and shoulders, throw socks into baskets, and dash back inside, trying to keep everything from getting soaked.

In families, certain needs must be satisfied. Clothing falls just below food and shelter in the hierarchy of importance. We must provide our children with clothes to wear, then make sure the clothes are clean. But depending on the technology and the number of children in a family, this task can be enormous, this washing-wringing-hanging-drying-folding-putting away of clothes. My mother could have written the Encyclopedia Britannica in the time she spent doing laundry.

Mom was called "Bess." She wasn't crazy about this nickname but she'd been called that most of her life. Her real name was Mary Elizabeth. That's what her mother always called her. But the name Bess started early. Mom's baby sister, Ruthie, couldn't pronounce the "th" in Elizabeth. It came out Elizabess, which became Bess, which stuck for seventy years.

Nicknames fly about wildly in families. For some reason neither of us can fathom or recall, Steve called me Twang. I hated this name. It made me feel like a hick and at the age of nine or ten I definitely did not want to be a hick. I got infuriated when he called me Twang, so of course he called me that all the time. He'd elongate the "a" horribly, slowly twisting the knife. "Hey, Twaaaaaang," he'd call to me in front of my friends.

For retribution I called him Wedge. I said his head looked like a golf club, like a wedge. Where I came up with that I have no idea. His head didn't look anything like a wedge. With his fat red cheeks his head looked more like a pumpkin or a butternut squash.

I always felt sorry for my mother, having to raise the pack of us. I watch friends now trying to cope with two children and I think: "How did she ever deal with six of us, especially us six, with us five boys." We were not a batch of Goldilocks.

Genghis Khans would be closer to the truth. There was always some battle going on. Susan and I yelled and clawed at each other. Steve threw tantrums. Johnny and Tom had wars.

A boy lived up the block for a time who none of the neighborhood kids could stand. He was arrogant, obnoxious, and stuck on himself. One day after school when I was in kindergarten, Steve and I ambushed him. We jumped out of a hedge, grabbed him and locked him in his garage. He went nuts. He yelled and screamed and pounded on the door. He said he'd get us when he got out. No one was home at his house so no one could hear him screaming and pounding on the inside of the garage door. We left him there for two hours. Finally, since it was nearly dinnertime, we figured we'd better let him out.

We snuck up to the door, pulled the stick out of the latch, and took off running. He heard us and shot out the door. It was like shaking up a jar of hornets and taking the top off. He saw us dash around the corner and chased after us. I zigzagged around trees and through yards but he caught up with me and hit me flush on the head with a hammer. I was knocked out cold and my head split open. Blood ran out like wine from a broken crock. Steve ran and told my mother. You can imagine her reaction when she saw me on the ground covered with blood. It wasn't as serious as it looked. I was fine, except for the stitches and a big scar on the top of my head that gradually disappeared years later.

How my mother survived our childhoods I often wonder. This was but one in an assembly line of traumas visited upon her by her darling and decorous children. One of us was always involved in some catastrophe or other. Fights, broken bones or bicycle crashes. One time Steve was playing touch football in the side yard and caught an errant elbow in the mouth. One of his upper teeth was growing in at an exaggerated angle above the regular line of his teeth. It cut clean through half of his upper lip like a knife through a veal cutlet. Off to the hospital. Tom and his pals had a contest in the locker room at the town swimming pool to see who could hold his breath the longest. Tom was so tenacious and competitive that he held his breath until he blacked out. He collapsed and broke his jaw when his face smashed against the concrete floor.

I had a talent for cutting my head open, which I seemed to do bloodily and often. When I was five or six I slipped in the bathroom at night and hit my head on the toilet bowl. It opened a terrible gash and I howled. My parents wrapped my bleeding head in a big towel and rushed me down to Doc Andrews' house, our family doctor, and roused him out of bed. The gash was too big to sew together with stitches. He had to close it with steel clamps. When he finished he wrapped the whole top of my head with white gauze until the bandage looked like a turban. I was well enough to go to school the next morning but talked my mother into letting me stay home. Everyone would laugh at me. I looked like a fool. And what could I tell my friends, that I'd split my head open on the toilet? She relented, but the next day I had to go and face the humiliation.

Every autumn we raked the fallen leaves into giant piles. Our parents thought of these piles as a safe way to burn the leaves. We thought of them as fun. We'd run and dive into them the way we dove headfirst into the big waves at Lake Michigan in the summertime. One year a mound of leaves was already started at the back of Stacy Smithson's yard, but it wasn't big enough to really enjoy. We all raked more leaves and piled them higher and higher until we built a great fluffy mountain. We'd back away, get a running start and dive headlong into the pile. This was indescribable bliss to us. What we didn't know was that at the bottom of the original mound of leaves was a concrete cinder block. My head discovered this fact in sudden and startling fashion. I ran home, my head wrapped in my bloody shirt, and surprised my mother. When she saw me I thought her heart would stop. After a few moments she gathered herself and rushed me down to Doc Andrews again, who by now was thinking of my scalp as quilting practice.

How do our mothers inure themselves to such shocks? We leave them dazed and breathless with upset, then two days later go back out and pull stunts crazier than the first ones. At the base of it they fear for our lives. This is the core of the terrible power that we as their children hold over them.

SNOWBALLS

I never questioned the existence of winter, the way I never questioned breathing, thunderstorms, or the inevitability of Steve's schemes to vex me. Winter was simply there, part of the annual cycle of seasons. It was not something one had a choice about. Only much later in life did I discover that people flee from winter (at least winter as we knew it in Michigan, with blizzards, ice storms, darkness at five o'clock, and temperatures of 15 degrees below zero). Fleeing is essentially what various ducks, geese, and other migratory birds have been doing since their species first quacked or honked their way across the autumn sky winging southward.

But winter also had its charms. Roaring fires in the fireplace. Sledding on the hills behind Billy Kern's house or ice skating on a rink we made by flooding the Smithson's backyard with a hose. There surely could be no Christmas — or Christmas presents — without winter, or so I believed in my ignorance of warm latitudes. Bing Crosby sang about White Christmases, and Bing played a priest, Father O'Malley, in The Bells of St. Mary's, so it must be true. No plagues of mosquitoes was a distinct benefit of winter, along with no Junebugs, snakes, poison ivy, or bats zooming through the air at dusk. But my favorite thing about winter was snowballs.

Snowballs were instant fun. Anytime, any place. You could throw them at your brother, your friends, or even better, at your older sister when you saw her walking home from school holding hands with her stupid boyfriend. Walking down the street or through a field in the wintertime, we just naturally reached down and packed a snowball as we ambled along. It was like kicking a stone on a gravel road in summer. And since you have a snowball in your hand, you have to find something to throw it at.

"See that garbage can across the street?" Steve would say. "Bet you a Tootsie Roll you can't hit it." This target possessed a particular allure because, being made of tin in those days, garbage cans made a loud clang if you hit them. I'd wind up and throw my hard-packed snowball with my best center fielder's arm. If I hit the garbage can, Steve had a chance to tie me. If I missed, he had to hit it himself to collect the Tootsie Roll. Stop signs were great targets because they were ubiquitous and bright red, so you could always tell exactly where your snowball hit. Even though slightly off-center, the "O" in the STOP was our bullseye, and whoever got closest to the O won.

Steve made the best snowball throw I ever saw. We walked the five blocks home from St. Robert's elementary school every day to eat lunch (another of my mother's favorite tasks, I'm sure). One day as we were walking back to school, packing our snowballs in our gloved hands as we went, we saw Bobby Asher's older sister, Janet, who was a senior at Flushing High, walking on the sidewalk across the street, slightly ahead of us. She was holding a brown paper bag in her left hand and reaching into the bag with her right.

Steve nudged me with his elbow and said, "Watch this."

He waited just a moment, then launched a high arcing throw into the winter air. Oblivious to us, Janet strolled on up the gentle incline of Hazelton Street. She withdrew her hand from the paper bag, holding half a sandwich made of white bread and cut on the diagonal from corner to corner. Peanut butter and jelly? Tuna fish salad? It was, as I recall, a Friday, and the Ashers were Catholics, too, so it couldn't have been beef or chicken (no meat on a Friday for us mackerel snappers). Janet raised the sandwich to take a bite and when it was no more than two inches from her open mouth, Steve's snowball crashed directly into her hand and knocked the sandwich into the snow bank. Janet screamed and the paper bag went flying. It was as though a cherry bomb had gone off in her hand.

At the same instant Steve and I said, "Wow!" We looked at each other and took off running around the corner, turning our heads away, hoping that Janet couldn't see our faces, because there would be hell to pay if she did. We didn't stop running for about four blocks, till we got all the way past Cherry Street and were sure Janet wasn't after us. We pulled up next to a huge oak tree, its limbs bare in winter.

SNOWBALLS

"Man, that was AMAZING!" I said. "That sandwich was right HERE!" and I held my hand just in front of my mouth. "Then BAM! Perfect." We both nearly collapsed on the ground laughing. But we also realized that we had to keep our mouths shut about this one, at least for awhile, or we would be real sorry. Janet had brothers. And they were big.

With any epicurean delight, the quality and consistency of the ingredients are crucial to the quality of the result. A delectable peach cobbler requires fresh, juicy, sweet peaches that are perfectly ripe, neither prematurely picked from the tree nor overripe and fermenting, a pastry crust with just the right amount of butter and moisture to bind the dough, and an oven that holds the proper temperature. The consistency of the snow, its moisture content, and the air temperature are key ingredients in making an ideal snowball. In the Colorado Rockies, ski resorts pray that loads of light, dry powder will drop from the sky. Dry powder is great for skiers, but hopeless for making snowballs. It's like trying to make a pie crust from dry flour — nothing binds or sticks together. But you also don't want snow that is too wet and heavy. Your snowballs will be slushballs, your gloves will get all wet, and the slushballs will break into pieces when you throw them. Not to mention that if you make a stash to assault Stacy Smithson's snow fort across the back fence and the temperature suddenly drops, they will turn to iceballs and hurt somebody.

Snowballs can be wonderfully practical objects, ideal

for scaring off howling tomcats in the middle of the night (in fact, keeping a batch stacked and ready on the outside window sill for just such contingencies is always a smart idea). Throwing snowballs during the long winter months is also a great way to keep your arm in shape for baseball.

But though snowballs are one of nature's most utilitarian, entertaining, and aesthetically pleasing objects, their purest and most reliable functions are to create mischief and torment adults.

On Hazelton Street in Flushing we lived directly across from the Methodist Church, which faced onto Main Street. When my brother, Mike, was a youngster an addition to the church was built. Mike and his pals (Sam, Gary, and Joe — last names withheld to protect the guilty) discovered, much to their delight, that the addition's back door never seemed to be locked. So at night they would sneak in, climb the stairs to the second floor, play, hang out, and generally revel in the purely illicit, forbidden joy of it all.

The addition's upstairs had a wide front window that overlooked Main Street, from which they could spy unseen on the activities below. When winter and the heavy snows arrived — snowball season — they concocted a perfect scheme. A row of large maple trees stood like sentinels in front of the church, between the sidewalk and the two-lane street. The boys each packed a cache of snowballs and hid behind one of the maple trees. When a car came by they would all leap out from behind the trees, pelt the car with snowballs, then run like mad down the side of the church. They would dart into the back door of the church addition, lock it from the inside, dash upstairs and look out the front window at the scene below. Almost invariably, the driver (usually a man, in those days) would slam on his brakes, jump out of the car, and yell like a banshee into the darkness or search vainly for the odious little demons who had bombarded his car. Some drivers got flashlights from their trunks and went searching behind hedges and between the houses. But the demons had always vanished. They were safe inside the church, upstairs, "laughing our butts off," as Mike once described it.

Gradually their raids grew bolder. One day a big storm left the ground blanketed in silent white. The snow had that perfect consistency snowballers crave. Mike and his pals made snowmen. They threw snowballs at each other, at stop signs, and at neighbors' dogs until well after dark. Then came an audacious idea: They rolled up two huge balls, as if for another snowman, two balls of snow nearly two feet in diameter each. But these were not for any snowman. Mike and Sam picked up one, Joe and Gary the other, to gauge the weight and bulkiness. They all grinned. Not bad. This could work.

They moved each ball behind one of the big maple trees in front of the Methodist church. Then they settled into their stations. Not many cars were on the streets this night because of all the new snow. They let a few go by so they could judge the speed and the distance away (just a few feet), and screw up their courage a bit—though they were laughing out loud at the sheer boldness of their plan.

It was time. "Here comes one," somebody said. They spied a lone pair of headlights coming down Main Street from the east, heading toward downtown. Each set of boys hefted their snowball in preparation. The car came closer. They started to slowly swing the snowballs back and forth, pendulum fashion, to build momentum. "Okay. One...two..." They swung the balls higher. "Three!!" Mike and Sam let go a mighty fling, as did Joe and Gary a split-second later. SPLAT! SPLAT! Two direct hits. One on the hood, the other near the windshield. "Yeow!!!" they yelled in celebration and took off running, down the side of the church to the addition's backdoor. Sam pulled the handle and—it didn't budge. He pulled again. "Holy Jesus! It's locked!" All four of them tugged and pulled, but the door refused to open. They heard a grown man's angry curses near the front of the church, then he was heading toward them. Panic hit and they took off running, with no place to hide.

    They ran across the back parking lot deep with snow and jumped a fence into the Farleys' backyard. They heard the man close on their trail, yelling at them. And he sounded MAD! Instinctively they split up, Mike and Sam going left through the backyards toward Cherry Street, Joe and Gary heading right toward Hazelton.

    Mike's lungs were burning. They cleared two more fences and his legs were heavy from running through the deep snow. Sam was a few yards ahead, but they both stumbled jumping over a picket fence. They picked themselves up, but Mike stumbled again as he tried to scramble forward, and Sam fell a little further on. Mike turned over in the snow and the man was looming over him, a huge dark hulk panting in the darkness. Mike could see the white clouds of his breath and felt terror run deep through his belly. He lay shaking in the snow, but not from cold.

"You little son-of-a-bitch. I oughta kick your ass right up on your shoulders! The both of you," the man said in a rage.

Mike thought the man was going to pick him up and hit him. But he didn't. He hovered over him for what seemed like eternity, then he muttered and kicked the snow. "Stupid damn kids," he said. Finally he turned and walked away. Then he stopped and Mike could see his silhouette pointing back at them. "Don't let me ever catch you pulling a stunt like that again. You hear? You think it's funny, but it's not. Somebody could get killed." He turned away again and trudged off through the darkness.

Mike and Sam lay on their backs in the snow. Mike looked up at the stars in the winter sky, but all he could see was that black silhouette, pointing back at him.

HELL

I was given a picture of hell as a child. It was not a photograph or painting. It was a mental picture, a sensory image imprinted inside me by Sister Angelica. Dear woman. The picture she gave me was vivid. I could virtually feel it. I could smell the burning flesh. Sister Angelica was a genius of communication. She should have been an actress. She kept her audience rapt with attention. And if your attention wandered, she rapped your knuckles with a wooden ruler. It is said we have no precise memory of pain, but my knuckles recalled the burning sting of that ruler for years afterward.

Sister Angelica taught us about hell, sin and eternity. We heard a lot about eternity. We would spend eternity either in heaven or in hell. Where we ended up was our choice. But whichever we chose, through the indicator of our earthly acts, the result would last a very long time. For all eternity. And we only had one crack at determining where we would spend it—this lifetime. There were no second chances, no reprieves. If we burned, we burned...forever.

"Hell is where you go if you commit a mortal sin," Sister Angelica said. "Do you know what hell is like, children?"

"No, Sister," we replied in unison. We were all six or seven years old.

"Let me tell you," she said. Which she did.

She was at her most lucid and clear, at her terrifying best. Hell was fire. Hell was flames and burning. She made us feel the fire. But the flames in hell would not consume our bodies. We would feel the pain, the searing of our flesh like a steak on a grill, but our own body would never burn up. We would go on burning, feeling that intolerable pain... forever.

"Have you ever burned your hand or fingers in a flame?" she asked.

Of course we all had—another instance where the body recollects its pain.

"Just imagine—and put on your thinking caps, children, really picture this—imagine if your hand got burned in a fire. Just think how much that hurts. How terrible that pain would be. But imagine how it would feel if you couldn't pull your hand out of the fire, if something held it there no matter how much you pulled and screamed."

We were all squirming in our chairs.

"And just think if not just your hand, but your whole body was thrown into that fire. And you couldn't get out. That your whole body felt that incredible pain and burning—your face and legs and arms, everything—but the fire didn't burn you up. You just went on burning and burning, feeling the pain, but you could never escape it. Never. Not for all eternity. That's what hell is like. That's what happens if you commit a mortal sin and die and go to hell."

She let this sink into the silence in the room for a while. Then she told us about eternity.

"Do you know how long eternity is, children?" she asked.

We didn't. We had no idea.

"You're six or seven years old now. Does that seem like a long time?"

It seemed like forever. Waiting for the school year to end seemed like forever two or three times over.

"Think about a beach, children, a long sandy beach where you can build sandcastles. Picture how long that beach is and how many millions of grains of sand are on that beach. Millions and millions. Billions. Now imagine that each grain of sand represents your whole lifetime, the amount of time you'll spend on this earth. If you took all the grains of sand, not just on that beach, but on all the beaches and in all the deserts in the whole world, the Sahara Desert and the Mojave Desert and Death Valley, and each grain of sand in all those places represented your lifetime, all that time, those millions and millions and billions of years, would be like a split second compared to how long eternity is. Eternity never ends. Ever. That's how long you'll burn in hell if you commit a mortal sin."

We shuddered.

I thought of the Sleeping Bear Sand Dunes up north and all the beaches down at Lake Michigan. They went on for miles. That was a lot of grains of sand.

Hell

I can't remember exactly when the nightmares started. I would wake up screaming in the middle of the night. The flames were all around me, burning me, crackling my flesh, never ending. I'd run from my bedroom screaming.

I remember my mother holding me in the light of the bathroom, trying to comfort me, trying to calm my terror. I couldn't stop screaming. All I could see were the flames, burning my flesh forever and ever and ever.

Finally I would calm down. I remember my mother stroking my head and my tears soaking into the flannel of her nightgown.

For years afterward whenever I walked on the beach at Lake Michigan looking for seagull feathers, or climbed the Sleeping Bear Dunes, I'd think of all those grains of sand and how long I'd burn if I committed a mortal sin.

ANIMAL CRACKERS

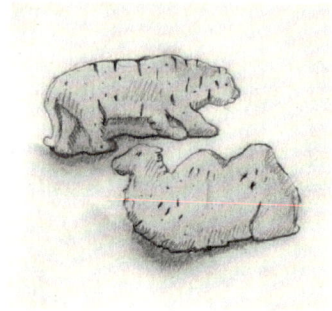

Existential psychology says that no cause and effect exists within the individual psyche—that events in our past don't cause behavior or reactions in the present. We have a history and a future, the existentialists say, but our actions exist only in relation to our present. I think of dentists and don't believe it.

I don't dislike dentists as people. In my rational mind, I even appreciate the importance of their work. We need our teeth. But I would rather be hung upside down by my toes in a wind storm than go to the dentist.

This aversion is wound through with memory and association. It is really an aversion to pain. I appreciate the dentist's dilemma: pain motivates our visits but he must inflict more pain to remedy our discomfort. This was especially true when I was little. Dental technology was not advanced then. There was no nitrous oxide, no high speed drills. In my memory the Novocain needles are eight inches long, even though I know better.

This aversion began when I was about seven years old, just into the Age of Reason. I had never been to the dentist before. On my first visit I didn't have a cleaning or a checkup — I had a tooth pulled. It was terrifying. Dr. Burnett was our dentist. He stood ramrod straight, a meticulously groomed man with never a hair out of place who triggers in my mind the picture of a crisp Robert McNamara. The part in his black-and-gray hair was as precise and straight as the cut of a razor.

Dr. Burnett was a technical master. Twenty years later other dentists told me that his fillings were among the best they'd ever seen. But to Dr. Burnett, pain deserved the attention of a gnat in the next room. Pain was a small, curious joke to him. He couldn't fathom the power it held over his patients, so he mostly ignored it. But if I squirmed or squealed too loudly, he used shame and guilt to quell the disturbance. He'd put down his pick or drill with a perturbed air and look me straight in the eye.

"Now, are you going to be a little man and let me do my work, or are you going to act like a baby?" he'd say.

He knew my weak spots. Having four older brothers and a big, strong dad, I didn't want to be called a baby. I wanted to be a man at the age of seven and make everyone proud of me. But with the pain in my mouth I bawled instead.

My mother took me to Dr. Burnett that first time because I had a terrible toothache. I'd never experienced such pain, except maybe with an earache. The left side of my mouth felt like it had a piece of shrapnel in it. Dr. Burnett probed around inside my mouth, causing lightning bolts of pain. A minute later I saw the needle. I felt a grip of terror. Thirty years later I remembered it as if it were last week. He stuck the needle in my mouth and it was so long I thought it would come out the back of my head.

At last the ordeal was finished. Dr. Burnett held a decayed "baby tooth" in his hand. I had a hole in my mouth that my tongue kept probing involuntarily.

But at least now I could look forward to Animal Crackers. A tradition existed in my family. After we'd gone to the dentist my mother took us out for a box of Animal Crackers. I loved Animal Crackers, especially the lions and elephants. Before we were even out the door of Dr. Burnett's office I said: "We go for the Animal Crackers now, don't we Mom?"

"Yes, we'll get you some Animal Crackers," she answered.

Animal Crackers

I knew the routine. I'd been in the car before when Mom picked up Susan or Steve or Tom from the dentist. There was a small market just down the street where she always stopped. Today we drove right past it. My head turned in disbelief as we drove by.

"But aren't we going to stop at—?" My voice trailed off.

"We'll go to downtown Flushing," she said. "We have some errands to do there."

Dr. Burnett's office was in Flint, the city about ten miles from Flushing. I contented myself with her response, and as we drove I kept biting my lower lip where I'd gotten the shot of Novocain. My lip felt like a piece of dead rubber. I could bite it or pinch it hard between my thumb and forefinger and barely feel a thing. It felt thicker than usual.

We drove down Flushing Road which became Main Street after we passed the city limits. We passed North Hazelton Street where we lived and headed toward downtown. I started getting excited again, thinking about my Animal Crackers. We were two blocks from the store when my mother slowed down and turned left—into Doc Andrews' driveway.

"What are we stopping for?" I said, mystified and a little alarmed. My mouth was starting to pound as the Novocain wore off.

"Oh, we just have to stop for a minute," she said, getting out of the car.

"But what about my Animals Crackers?"

"We'll get them in a little while. Let's go inside."

"What for?"

"We just have a few little things to do."

A few little things to do. I was suddenly filled with foreboding that this somehow involved me. I reluctantly got out of the car. It was not unusual that we'd stop here. This was not only Doc Andrews' office, but also the family home. His wife, Melba, was one of my mother's best friends. Their youngest son, Zell, was a pal of mine, and their other kids, Curry, Delno, and Marietta, were friends of my various brothers or my sister.

But we didn't go to the back door of the house. Mom walked into the office. I didn't like the looks of this. As soon as we were inside, the reason for our stop became clear. I was here for a polio shot. Mom even had an appointment. I felt tricked and betrayed. I'd had enough needles for one day. I wanted my Animal Crackers. But before I could say much the nurse came out and swept me into the examination room. A few minutes later Doc Andrews appeared.

"So, how are we doing today?" Doc Andrews said in his good-natured way.

"I've just been to the dentist. He pulled a tooth and put this big needle in my mouth and now Mom brings me here," I said petulantly, as if I'd undergone torture.

Doc Andrews smiled.

"Well, this will be like a picnic compared to the dentist. And we'll be through before you know it."

He was right, of course. But when he stuck the needle in my right arm I had to wince dramatically as if I'd been run through with a sword. I was feeling persecuted and sorry for myself.

"There now, that wasn't so bad, was it?" he said.

"It wasn't great."

"It sure beats getting polio." He had a point there. "And look at it this way. Instead of ruining two days, you get the dentist and your polio shot out of the way in one afternoon."

The tragedy of the day was that I never got my Animal Crackers. By the time we finished it was too late to go to the store. To top it off, I played baseball for an hour after getting the polio shot, and with all the throwing my right arm throbbed for three days.

So now, just to right the injustice, whenever I go to the dentist, I go out afterward and buy myself a box of Animal Crackers.

Fishing

In 1952, when I was three, my parents bought an old cottage in northern Michigan. It was on Platte Lake, between the villages of Beulah and Honor. The cottage was built near the turn of the century from logs that were floated across the lake from the north shore, then milled into boards.

Platte Lake became a part of my blood and spirit. Its seasons, peace, the modulations of its spring and autumn sounds are woven into my picture of the world: flocks of geese honking in October, the still hush of falling snow, thunder booming like a shotgun, crickets chirping in the summer darkness.

When I was little Mom and Dad packed the lot of us—six kids and the dog, Winky—into our old Packard and headed "up north" the day after school was out. We stayed all summer until Labor Day, except for my Dad—who drove the four hours up and back each weekend—and whichever of my brothers who were old enough to work summer jobs.

I went fishing almost every day. I fished from our boat out in front of the cottage or at the end of the lake. I fished in the creek down the way or from docks up and down the shoreline. All the neighbors knew me and humored my eccentric fishing habits. No one ever fished from the docks except me and occasionally one of my brothers who I dragged along. What could you catch from a dock, the end of which was thirty feet from shore in two feet of water? But I caught things—perch and sunfish and rock bass and bluegills. I crept silently onto the dock boards in my bare feet, sometimes crawling on my hands and knees so the fish wouldn't see my shadow and be scared away. I moved with the stealth of a burglar. Since I was too small to go out in the boat by myself, I usually had no choice but to fish from the docks. Or I fished out on the lake with Steve or my Dad or Bob Norin or Mr. Harpst or Lee Collins, the nephew of a neighbor.

"Had any bites yet, Lee?"
"A couple little perch is all, nibbling."
"Little perch. I'd rather get no bites than them. They just steal your worm and keep the bigger fish away."

The end of Lee's pole bobbed up and down, as if it were someone's finger sending Morse Code.

"Look. There they go again," he said. "Trying to get my worm."

He yanked the pole upward to snatch the bait from the pests hidden twenty feet below, then let the line settle back a few feet farther to the right.

For three or four minutes the rod was still. Lee looked at me in the bow of the boat.

"I wonder if they got it," he said.

I raised my eyebrows in question and Lee began reeling in his line. "Darn," he said. The hook was bare.

"Maybe we should move," I said. "Go down to the end of the lake by the weed bed. We'd catch something there."

Lee dug through the can of damp leaves looking for another nightcrawler.

"No, we'd better stay here," he said finally. "I promised your dad we'd stay in front of the cottages and come in at sunset so you can go to the drive-in movie with everybody."

Normally, I loved going to the Cherry Bowl Drive-in, but tonight I wasn't too excited. My brother, Steve, Mike Bishop and I were being taken there by Susan and her new boyfriend, who would probably try to put his arm around her all night. I'd rather fish.

"There's still a good hour left before the sun goes down, maybe more," I said. "We could pull up anchor, go down to the weed bed for awhile and get in by sunset easy. It's only a couple of miles. I don't know if I can stand another hour of these little perch."

Lee baited his hook and dropped it back into the water. "You'll live," he said.

A few minutes later Lee got a bite. He started reeling it in, and after a second knew exactly what it was—another little perch. It had the weight of a hummingbird dancing at the end of his line. He took the hook carefully from its mouth, but rather than dropping the small fish over the side of the boat, he tossed it far over his shoulder. Forty feet away it hit the water with a tiny splash.

"Maybe now he won't be able to find my worm again," he said, perturbed.

"Did you see the two smallmouth bass Mr. Nathan caught this morning?" I said.

Lee was digging through the can of damp leaves.

"No, were they big ones?"

"Big? They were monsters. Both almost five pounds."

"Five pounds!" exclaimed Lee. "What kind of bait was he using?"

"Worms."

"Where did he catch them?"

"Down by the weed bed."

"Pull up the anchor, Pete. Let's go."

Lee cut the motor, letting the boat glide silently the last thirty yards as we approached the weed bed. He had a theory about noisy motors scaring the fish away which sometimes exceeded reason. Even in a hundred feet of water he insisted on cutting the motor early.

We both peered into the lake, looking for the drop-off where the leafy-topped plants became barely visible from the deeper water. This was where the "big ones" lurked, or so the catches of old Mr. Nathan suggested.

Mr. Nathan was a legend on Platte Lake. For forty-five years he had been plucking prize fish from these waters with the skill of a black bear in a mountain stream, even when no one else could catch a thing. Other fishermen did everything to learn his tricks. They tracked him with binoculars, then tried to duplicate his movements. But they could never match him and he loved to keep them guessing.

To pique his jealous watchers further, after cleaning his bigger catches, Great Northern and Walleye pikes, bass and even a muskie now and then, he would nail the huge heads onto the telephone pole in front of his house. Fishermen would detour down the gravel road and gape in awe at these prizes. He never revealed his secrets and always fished alone, except two or three times each summer when he took Lee and me along. We were his favorite kids on the lake. This was how Lee got the seed of his noisy motor theory.

"Okay, Pete, drop it," Lee said. He could see the tops of the weeds and determined the boat was in just the right spot. I slipped the anchor silently into the water and when it hit the bottom, cinched up the rope.

"Five pounds," Lee said with wonder as we baited our hooks.

"I swear to God, Lee. They were real beauties."

"Boy, what I'd give to catch a five-pound smallmouth bass. Can you imagine the battle he'd give you?"

"It must be like having a bronc on your line."

Thirty minutes later all the five-pound smallmouths seemed to be elsewhere, along with the sunfish, rock bass and bluegills. We hadn't had a single bite.

"Maybe this wasn't such a hot idea after all," he said.

"Well, we don't have those stupid little perch stealing

our worms every two minutes."

"At least they kept us awake."

"Kept you awake. I was awake already. Hey? Did you see that? Something jumped over there."

Lee turned to see the concentric ripples moving on the surface. Beyond, the sky was beginning to redden.

"Was it big?"

"I couldn't tell, but it made a good splash. Maybe we'll start to get some action."

"We'd better get some action pretty soon. The sun's starting to—"

"Hey," I said. "I felt something." I straightened up and held the rod still, feeling for the slightest touch. Suddenly the end of the pole dipped. I yanked on it and started reeling in the line.

"We've got a keeper this time and he's not a stupid little perch."

"It's probably his mother."

I hadn't hooked a large fish, but it was giving me a good fight.

"What do you think it is?" Lee said. "I say it's a medium-sized rockie."

"Nope. It's too quick for a rockie. I bet you an ice cream it's a little smallmouth."

A few minutes later we were both surprised. I'd caught a large bluegill.

"Well, what'dya know?" said Lee.

We seldom caught bluegills, with their lustrous blue-green color and gold bellies. But they were delicious eating. My Mom loved bluegills and this one was a beauty. I took it off the hook, carefully ran the metal stringer clip behind the lower lip where it didn't hurt the fish, and slipped the stringer overboard. The fish could swim about but not get away.

"Bluegills swim in schools. Maybe we'll get some more," said Lee.

The action got fast. In the next 15 minutes we caught three more and a rock bass.

"This is what I call fishing," I said.

Suddenly Lee got a thunderous strike. He yanked up his rod and it bent over double. The reel handle whacked his knuckles and the fish shot off with his line.

"Get the net! Get the net!" he yelled, though he barely had control of the reel. I scrambled for the net and almost fell out of the boat in my excitement.

Lee pulled on his rod and it curved in a vicious arc.

"Man, this thing is huge! It must be 10 pounds, 15 pounds!"

The fish moved furiously away, darting left and right, then headed for deeper water. Lee pulled against it, wanting to keep it closer, and the big fish turned back, coming toward the boat. Quickly Lee reeled in the slack line so the fish couldn't throw the hook. The fish turned again, bolting for the deep water. Lee put some drag on the line and SNAP! He nearly fell over backward. Just as fast as it had come, the big fish was gone.

"Oh, no!" I yelled, jumping up and down. I wanted to dive in after it. "What happened? Did he break the line?"

"I guess so. There wasn't any slack. Just boom, and he's gone." Lee was in a state of shock. He sat in silence for a moment, then dejectedly reeled in the rest of his line.

"That fish was huge. I mean huge!" I said. "Did you see the way it bent your pole?"

"See it? You should have felt it. Talk about having a bronc on your line." He shook his head. "Nobody will ever believe this," he said, and finished reeling in his line.

"Holy cow!" Lee exclaimed.

"What?"

"Look at this." He held something up for me to see in the dim twilight. It was his hook—bent almost straight.

"That fish bent the hook? I can't believe that."

We looked at each other, dumbfounded.

"I wonder what it was?" I said.

"I don't know, but it was bigger than a five-pound smallmouth. That thing could eat a five-pound smallmouth."

"Hey," I said slowly, my eyes widening. "You don't suppose..." My voice trailed off.

"I don't suppose what?"

"That it was that big muskie Mr. Nathan's been trying to catch?"

Lee's eyes got bigger too.

"The one he hooked last June, that got away right before he could land it?"

"Yeah. He told us he hooked it right at this end of the lake, remember? Just out from the drop-off."

I felt like we'd just looked a lion straight in the face.

A rattling noise at the front of the boat pulled us from our trance. When I had gone for the net I had hooked my rod under the seat and in all the excitement had forgotten it completely. Now it was bobbing up and down. I dashed to the bow and in a few minutes we had another rock bass on the stringer.

"Hurry up and rig your line again, Lee. They're really biting. But don't lose that bent hook."

"What do you think, I'm some kind of flathead?"

In the next two hours it seemed like we had a fish on the line all the time. Both stringers were full and we even threw back fish that were normally keepers. We were in heaven on Platte Lake.

Something hit my bait hard.

"Wow, this guy's a battler," I said.

The fish was nothing compared to Lee's lost giant, but it was good-sized and a fighter. It darted and pulled. When it streaked unexpectedly under the boat, bending my rod nearly double, I had to struggle to keep the line from getting tangled in the anchor rope.

"I'll bet you that ice cream this one's a smallmouth," I said.

"How about I bet you it's not a little perch."

"Very funny."

When I grabbed the line a foot above the splashing fish and hoisted it into the boat it wasn't a smallmouth we saw.

"What's that?" I said.

Lee turned on his flashlight so we could see better.

"Holy cow, it's a catfish," Lee yelled.

I dropped the fish as though I'd been holding a tarantula. We both jumped backward and the catfish went flopping into the bottom of the boat.

"Watch out for its whiskers! They'll sting you bad," Lee said.

Fishing

    We watched from on top of the seats as the fish flopped about in the stream of light. It was smooth, shiny and black, with long whiskers on its chin.

    "I've never caught a catfish before. What do you do with it?" I asked.

    "You've got to get the hook out of its mouth."

    "What do you mean I have to get the hook out of its mouth?"

    "Well, it's your fish," said Lee.

    I looked at the catfish for a minute.

    "They sure are ugly, aren't they?" I said.

    Just then we heard the vague hum of an engine and saw a spotlight moving across the water a hundred yards away. The engine was cut and in the silence we heard voices calling.

    "Leeeee......Peeeete.... Are you there?"

    We looked at each other in the faint glow from the flashlight. The catfish was still wriggling.

    "Is that us they're calling?" Lee said.

    "It sounds like it."

    "It almost sounded like your brother, Mike."

    "Leeeee....Peeeete....," the voice called again. "Can you hear me?"

    "Yeah. We're over here," Lee called back, shining his light toward the voices.

    We heard the engine start up. A few minutes later my older brother, Mike, and Sam Reeber, his buddy from down the shore, glided up in Sam's boat.

    "Are you two all right?" Mike asked anxiously.

    "All right? Of course we're all right. Why?" I asked.

"Why? The whole shore's out looking for you! You were supposed to be in three hours ago."

Lee and I looked at each other and it hit us both at once.

"The drive-in!" I said.

"Yeah, the drive-in," said Mike.

"I completely forgot."

"Just like I always said—the brain of a turnip. You're gonna wish you'd remembered when Dad gets ahold of you. Mom's a wreck. She's sure you both drowned."

"Have you been fishing all this time?" Sam asked.

"Yeah. You wouldn't believe how the fish have been biting. It's been incredible. Look."

We held up the two full stringers and the catfish.

"You caught all of those?" Sam exclaimed in disbelief.

"And probably another dozen just as big that we threw back," Lee said.

Mike looked at Sam and chuckled. "If they were biting like that, I'd have forgotten the drive-in too."

The shoreline was aglow with lights as we approached. Groups of people clustered together and I could see my mother pacing frantically back and forth. Lee's parents sat in two lawn chairs holding each other's hands.

"We found them! We found them! They're fine!" Mike yelled from the blackness of the lake about eighty yards off shore.

There was a moment of utter stillness. Then people streamed onto the dock to greet the two boats. A geyser of

FISHING

relief erupted as our parents hugged us, wiped tears from their eyes and felt their world come back together. In the midst of it all, my mother looked both of us sternly in the eyes.

"Do you realize what trouble and worry you caused everyone? We thought you'd drowned. Do you realize that?"

Lee and I looked sheepishly at the ground. "Yes, Ma'am," we said together.

"Don't you two ever pull another stunt like that."

The next day there was a huge fish fry with the catch of the night before. Neighbors brought fresh corn, vegetables, potato salad and applesauce. Already a mythology was growing about the fish so big it bent Lee's hook straight.

Old Mr. Nathan inspected the hook for awhile, then took Lee and me aside where no one else could hear.

"What do you think, Mr. Nathan?" Lee asked.

"Well, kids, I think it just may have been my old friend, the Muskie."

"Really."

"Yes, I do. And do you know what that means?"

"What?"

"It means that now he's our fish. And we'll go after him together."

HOLY ORDERS

I decided early to become a priest. It was a considered, manly decision, made with the deliberate self-examination that attends such choices. I was six years old.

Holy Orders was the sacrament of the priesthood. It was one of the sacraments you received only once in life, like Baptism and Extreme Unction. I hadn't received many sacraments at this point. I hadn't even reached the Age of Reason. I had only been baptized, which happens involuntarily at the age of about two weeks. Baptism is like an Eternal Soul-Life Insurance Policy. If you die in the first seven years of life you go straight to heaven, guaranteed. Not a bad trade for enduring a few sprinkles of water on the forehead. We Catholics didn't even have to suffer through getting dunked in a cold river the way the Baptists did.

I couldn't decide what kind of priest I wanted to be, though I knew I didn't want to be a missionary. I hated snakes and bugs, and missionaries were always sent off to a jungle somewhere. Maybe I'd start simple. I'd begin as a parish priest in some small town like Flushing, say lots of masses and hear confessions, then later become a cardinal. Going to Rome and wearing a red cap appealed to me.

My first gesture toward Rome took place that same year. I was in the first grade at St. Robert's Catholic School. The nuns lived in a large white convent next door to the rectory at the top of Cherry Street. Autumn arrived and the huge maple trees surrounding the convent dropped their bounty of leaves. Since I was going to be a priest and priests do good works, I offered to rake the nuns' yard. They offered to pay me. I said no, no, no. I wouldn't hear of it. In my heart this was an offering to God.

After a few days of raking leaves after school I didn't feel so righteous. The yard was gigantic. There were mountains of leaves. How could I be such an idiot, offering to rake the whole thing, alone? Six-year-olds, I discovered about myself, don't rake very fast.

The nuns were all smiles. They thought this yard-raking was stupendous. I kept thinking: maybe I'll spend two less years in purgatory when I die. I had to finish the job. I had committed myself and couldn't stop in the middle—a Damm didn't do that—though I desperately wanted to. While I was here raking leaves every day my buddies were playing tag and dodgeball. I worked faster and faster, despite the blisters on my hands.

After what seemed like two durations of eternity, I finished. I felt like a released prisoner. But I also felt proud. The yard looked beautiful. I decided that I still wanted to be a priest, but I was glad that I wouldn't be starting right away. These good works could be a burden.

The nuns were thrilled, probably because they didn't have to rake the yard themselves. As I slaved away I wondered if they were inside playing cards or watching Sky King on TV. When I finished they all gathered around to thank me. Sister Angelica handed me a small wrapped present. I blushed, and she said to open it. I shyly pulled off the ribbon and paper and opened the hinged box. Inside was a rosary. "I already have two rosaries," was my first thought. Then I thought, "Some priest you're going to make. Show a little gratitude." But this wasn't just any rosary, Sister Angelica told me. It was very special. The beads were a coffee brown color and the arms of the cross flared out at the ends. But the rosary was special for another reason. It had been personally blessed by Pope Pius XII. When Sister Angelica told me this I was stunned into silence. I wanted to kneel down in reverence.

"I can't take this, Sister," I said.

"We want you to have it."

"But, Sister—"

She held up her hand. I knew I'd better shut up and take it. I didn't want to incite her legendary wrath.

I treasured the rosary. It made me feel holy. Blessed by the Pope! I could scarcely believe such a thing, and that this rosary was mine. Every day after school I took it from its special place in my drawer and touched it, looked at it.

One day I came home and discovered the rosary's cross was gone. The small metal link was bent sideways. I went into a panic, then into a rage. I ran to my mother, bawling. No one admitted the crime. Weeks later I discovered that my brother Tom had taken it. He was in high school and it was "cool" to wear a cross around your neck on a chain. That was the style. By the time I found out, he had already lost it.

"How could you do that? Give it back to me," I screamed at him.

"I can't. I lost it. Besides, it's only a stupid cross. I'll get you another one."

"It's not the same. It was blessed by the Pope!"

"Oh, screw the Pope!"

"I'll tell Mom you said that." I didn't know what "screw the Pope" meant, but I figured the Pope wouldn't enjoy it. But I never told Mom and he never got me a cross. I still wanted to be a priest but I didn't show him priestly forgiveness. I wanted to smash his toes with a hammer. I had a ways to go in my quest for holiness.

I always thought that Holy Orders was a weird name for a sacrament. I couldn't make out its meaning. It sounded militaristic to me — soldiers got "orders" from superior officers. But maybe that was the intended connection. Priests were the "soldiers" of Christ, waging a holy war against sin and evil, their ammunition good works, prayer and sacrifice. They even wore uniforms — the collar and black cassock — to identify their allegiance.

Perhaps my desire to be a priest was linked to my name. St. Peter was my patron saint. Peter, the Rock. "And upon this Rock I will build my Church," Christ had said. Peter was a simple man, a fisherman. So was I. I fished for rock bass and bluegills from the docks at Platte Lake almost every day in the summer. I felt it was dictated in my lineage from St. Peter that I become a priest, that I carry on his calling.

"Son of a bitch! Goddamnit!"

This was not me speaking. It was Father Bush, our parish priest. I was an altar boy at Holy Family in Grand Blanc, twelve years old. We had just finished saying Saturday morning mass and were in the furnace room at the school, investigating some malfunction. Father Bush stood up and hit his head on a pipe. I wondered where he'd picked up such language. Not in the seminary, I figured, but then the seminary was thirty years ago for him.

If Father Bush hadn't been a priest, he'd have been a promoter or real estate tycoon. He was an extrovert, a man of flair, wit, and style. There was nothing remotely fuzzy-edged about him. His voice, laughter and opinions were as clear and sharp as a mountain bell. Rumor said he came from a well-to-do family, that he had money of his own. The priestly vow of poverty was certainly nowhere in evidence. He drove a jet black Buick Riviera and enjoyed playing golf at the country club (where I later worked as a caddy, then on the grounds crew, mowing greens and raking sand traps). If there was such a thing as a well-dressed priest, Father Bush was it. He was always impeccably groomed in his blacks and collar, ramrod straight and handsome. The lines of his life were like that—sharp, definite and defined.

And, if he was stylish and witty, he was also thoroughgoing in his devotion to Christ and his priestly duties. He said masses, gave sermons, heard our confessions, visited the sick, buried the old people and married the young. He raised money through bingo games and fish fries, built schools and was devoted to the children. He was a master builder and master fundraiser. When Father Bush took over the parish it possessed almost no facilities. There was an old church and little else. He raised the money and built a school, then a new church, a school addition, a rectory and a parish hall. He instituted a basketball team and numerous activities. He made possible our Catholic education (for better or worse).

I wondered later how Father Bush affected my view of the priesthood. He was not a contemplative man of quiet piety, not the archetypal priest. I could picture him more easily in Monaco than Rome. But he was also not the priest of my early childhood. That was Father Jacobs, who is amorphous in my memory. I remember him with his head slightly bent and his hands folded in silent prayer upon the altar. His assistant, Father Fedewa, was a young priest just out of the seminary. His hands were pressed together yet more earnestly in prayer, so earnestly in fact that his elbows flared straight out, as if he were doing isometric exercises for his chest muscles.

As the years passed, my resolve toward the priesthood weakened. This began in the fourth grade. I fell in love with Sally Jackson. At night I prayed that we'd get married when we grew up. During the day we passed notes in school. "I'll love you till all the little perch turn into smallmouth bass," I'd write, thinking this was very romantic. This love affair created a dilemma for me. I still wanted to be a priest, prayed that I'd marry Sally Jackson, and knew that priests couldn't marry. I decided finally that everything would work out all right. I must be going through "a phase"—kids were always going through phases, according to adults—and this interest in girls would pass. Strangely, it didn't.

TIGERS

Now and then Dad would drive us down to a Tigers baseball game in Detroit. We would leap excitedly into the old Packard for the hour and a half drive to Briggs Stadium (later called Tiger Stadium and widely considered one of the great ballparks in the country). Steve and I always felt like we were off to the sacred cathedral. But it wasn't the Cathedral of Mary or Joseph or St. Sebastian. It was the Cathedral of Baseball. The Big Leagues. The Majors. The shrine either of us would give our left arm to play in one day. Those rare games watching the Tigers in person must have tasted bittersweet to Dad, I realized years later. His lifelong dream, all the way through semi-pro ball, was to play in the Big Leagues himself. I don't remember him ever voicing this dream explicitly, but I knew it existed as surely as the leaves changed in autumn.

These pilgrimages to Briggs Stadium were in the

mid-Fifties and early Sixties, the days before the expansion and dilution in Major League Baseball. The American and National Leagues each had eight teams. The Giants and Dodgers were moving West from New York, but we neither noticed nor cared. They played in the National League and where we came from no one cared a fig about the National League.

We never got to sit behind home plate or near the dugouts, but we were still in heaven. We loved arriving early enough to watch batting practice and see the players shag fly balls in the outfield, but the magic really began when the extra players left the field and the starters took "infield." Infield was a baseball ritual as graceful and precise as a Margot Fonteyn and Rudolf Nureyev ballet. It touched some aesthetic chord deep inside me. During infield one of the coaches stands at home plate and hits a ground ball to the third baseman, who catches the ball and fires to first as if throwing out a runner. The first baseman then whips it back to the third baseman standing on the bag, who throws hard to the catcher, who whips it back down to first, then it's back to third and on to the catcher again, who now flips the ball casually to the coach standing at home plate. The coach hits a grounder to the shortstop and the progression begins anew, but each time with a yet more complex pattern of throws crisscrossing the infield like arrow shots. Short to first to home to second to third to home, all with the grace of dancers. I could watch pro baseball players take infield endlessly, fascinated, the way that years later I could watch Natalia Makarova do leaps—both were marvels I never tired of.

We were ardent fans of the Tigers players of that era: silky second baseman Frank Bolling; lanky right-handed pitcher Jim Bunning, so tenacious in big games; Charlie Paw Paw Maxwell; tobacco-chewing Harvey Kuenn, fearless in the field and at the plate. We loved Kuenn even after he was swapped heads up, player-for-player, for Cleveland's glamour slugger, Rocky Colavito, in one of the decade's biggest trades, because in our hearts Harvey would always be a Tiger.

But Steve and Dad and I shared a particular devotion to Al Kaline, the Tigers' spectacular—and eventual Hall of Fame—right fielder. As a 20-YEAR-OLD in 1955 Kaline hit .340 to win the major league batting title. This feat made him the youngest batting champion in American League history (edging out baseball immortal Ty Cobb, also a Detroit Tiger, who was so good that he ended his playing days with the highest career batting average of all time). Kaline was a magician in the outfield. He won ten Gold Gloves, the award given to the best-fielding player in the league at each position. In 1958, he had only two errors in 341 chances for a .994 fielding percentage, and had 23 outfield assists (runners thrown out on the bases), a ridiculously high total.

To this day I remember two events at Briggs Stadium as if they happened last Friday. The first involved Al Kaline. We were sitting far out in the right field stands (a LONG way from home plate, but the seats were cheap and close to Kaline's position). The Tigers were playing the Boston Red Sox with the incomparable Ted Williams, who many baseball aficionados still consider the greatest pure hitter in history. In 1941 Williams batted .406 over the course of an entire season, the last batter to break the hallowed .400 plateau.

In the middle of a tight game, Williams stepped to the plate with a runner on first and one out. After taking a few pitches, he ripped a searing line drive toward the right field seats. Kaline was playing deep and was off like a shot at the crack of the bat, but the ball was hooking hard away from him and he had NO chance to make a play. At the last second he made a desperate leap and somehow, only God knows how, he speared the ball high above the wall to steal a home run from Williams. He crashed into the fence, kept the ball in his glove, and in one unfathomable, impossible motion, spun in a counter-clockwise circle while falling to the ground and unleashed a 250-foot strike to first base to double off the runner, who'd been sprinting toward second, positive the ball could never be caught. Ted Williams, one of baseball's most intense and imperious players, stood stoic and grim on the grass behind first base, staring out at Kaline, as if unable to conceive that this line shot of a drive, sure to be a homer or at worst a double, had instead become, through this display of sheer athletic genius, an inning-ending double play. Seen through the prism of my child's memory, it remains the greatest play on a baseball diamond I have ever witnessed. (I wasn't at The Polo Grounds, of course, for Willie Mays' catch on Vic Wertz's drive to center.)

The other event I vividly recall occurred at a Yankees game. We hated the Yankees with a passion like that of the French for the Germans after WWII. The Yankees ALWAYS won the pennant. The Yankees ALWAYS won the World Series. Yogi Berra, Mickey Mantle, Billy Martin,

Whitey Ford—they could all go straight to hell as far as I was concerned (though I never would have harbored such a thought in my CONSCIOUS Catholic mind—then I would have to tell the priest in confession, and who knows, he might be a closet Yankee fan and I would be saying Hail Marys for hours).

This particular day Dad got us to the stadium good and early. The stands were nearly empty as we watched the Yankee players stretch and jog in the outfield, take batting practice and shag fly balls. We were sitting in the fifth or sixth row on the field level, far out along the third baseline, not quite to the left field corner. Steve and I always took our gloves to ballgames in the fervent hope that one day we might catch a home run or foul ball (though we knew the odds were long). As we sat pounding our gloves, the batting practice pitcher stood on the mound behind his protective screen and threw pitch after pitch to the batters. Suddenly a towering fly ball headed our way. Steve and I scrambled over the empty seats. The ball landed just out of my reach and careened back over our heads. We dashed toward it and just as I was about to grasp the ball, Steve, fatboy brutish lout bully that he was, elbowed me aside and stole the prize. He leaped with joy and exclamation, and I slunk crestfallen back to my seat. I was SO close to getting a ball that real big leaguers had thrown and played with. I couldn't share Steve's boundless excitement and sat dejected in my seat. Dad both congratulated Steve and rubbed my head in consolation.

A few minutes later, as I was staring enviously at Steve's treasure, I heard someone say, "Hey....Hey, kid," then a whistle. We all looked up and one of the Yankee players was standing on the grass about fifteen feet from the stands, motioning someone toward him. I looked all around, but we were the only people for several rows. I looked back at him and he pointed directly at me, then motioned me down. I numbly pointed my index finger at my chest—Who, me?—and he nodded.

"He wants you," Dad said to me. "He wants you to go down there. Go ahead."

"Me?" I said disbelievingly.

"Yes. Go ahead," he answered and nudged me toward the aisle.

Shyly I walked down the steps toward the field, my baseball glove on my left hand—where it had resided for much of my waking and sleeping life since about age three, like a naturally grown appendage. As I neared the railing the player pulled a ball from his glove and tossed it to me.

"That's for you, chief," he said and gave me a smile. I looked down and there it rested in my glove. A real major league baseball! It was not a dream, not a mirage. I looked back up at the tall, slender, but powerful-looking player standing before me in his Yankee road uniform.

"Wow! Thanks!" I called to him.

He winked at me, then trotted off to shag more flies.

I raced back up to Dad and Steve, barely able to breathe from excitement.

"Dad! Look! Look!" I said, clutching the ball in front of me like the Hope Diamond. We all touched and inspected and rubbed the ball, the high seams sewn with red thread. It was probably originally a game ball, then used for batting practice. But the fact that it was not brand new and spotless made it even more precious to me, because it had been pitched and hit and thrown by big league ballplayers. By the New York Yankees, no less. Steve, to his credit and my eternal surprise, was not petulant and jealous, but was as excited as I was. Dad reached in his pocket and took out an ink pen.

"Why don't you see if he'll sign it for you?" he said. I looked at him aghast and fearful.

"I couldn't bother him like that. He's all the way across the field. How would I even get his attention?"

"He'll be back over this way. I bet if you waited down by the railing and called to him when he came nearby, he might come over and sign it for you."

Such an action required much cogitation and screwing up of courage. Finally I decided to give it a try. I went down, leaned on the rail, and watched tall number 39 as he jogged leisurely across the field and caught the occasional fly ball. After a few minutes he was back near the left field line.

"Sir! Sir!" I called and waved to him. He saw me and trotted over.

"What can I do for you, chief?" he asked.

"Sir, I wondered if…if you might sign my baseball," I said, holding out the ball and the ink pen.

"I'd be glad to," he said. He took the ball and pen, carefully wrote his name, then handed them back to me. "There you go, chief. I gotta go now. We've got a game to play. But you do me a favor, okay? You keep your glove on, and practice every chance you get. Practice and practice and practice. And when you play, always play hard, just like you were in the Big Leagues. Okay?"

"Yes, sir," I said.

He rubbed the top of my head, then jogged off again, this time toward the Yankees' dugout, as the entire team was clearing the field. I ran back up to our seats, being careful not to smear the ink till it dried. When I got there we all looked at the ball. "Jim Coates" it said, in a very legible cursive script. We looked him up in the program.

"James Alton Coates. Pitcher. Throws right. Bats right. 6'4", 192 lbs. Born August 4, 1932, Farnham, Virginia."

From that day forward I didn't hate the Yankees quite so much, at least not until 1962 when they traded Jim Coates to the Washington Senators. My signed baseball rested proudly atop my dresser and for years I followed Jim Coates' career in the box scores of the Detroit Free Press. He pitched in the big leagues for nine seasons with four different teams. His record in 1959 with the Yankees was 6-1 with a 2.87 ERA in 100 innings, and 11-5 in 1961 with a 3.44 ERA. Not too shabby, as the saying goes. Even now, fifty-plus years later, I can see his slender form and the smile on his face as he tossed that ball my way.

Baseball — and occasionally fishing — were the principal ways I connected with my father. He wasn't always easy to approach or talk to. He would come home from the office, sit in his big chair in the living room, and disappear behind the pages of The Flint Journal, the local afternoon newspaper. After a day of legal or political wrangles you could tell he wanted time to disconnect, rejuvenate, to gather his strength before being hauled into the bedlam of his often frantic household. As a child I didn't understand this. It sometimes seemed like rejection. But I knew I could always ask him for a tip on my batting stance or fielding balls hit into the gap. Sometimes we would sit in the living room or on the front porch at the cottage listening to Ernie Harwell and George Kell broadcast Tiger games on the radio. I remember him teaching me how to bunt in the backyard at the farm.

"When you square around to bunt, you want to slide your right hand up the bat to about the trademark. Use only your thumb and index finger to hold the bat from the back side, and curl your other three fingers into your palm, like this," he would say, demonstrating. "That way, if the pitch hits the bat near your hand, you don't get your fingers broken. Then—and this is the most important thing—hold the bat real loose in your hands. Real loose. You deaden the ball that way and won't hit it too hard back to the pitcher or one of the infielders."

Whenever I squared around to bunt during a game, I repeated in my mind like a mantra, "Loose. Real loose." It was almost like Dad was there at the plate with me. And I became a damn good bunter.

Putsy

My parents hated cats. This attitude was akin to racism. Neither of them had ever been around a cat. Their feelings were born of hearsay. "Cute little kittens turn into cats," they'd been told. Cats were aloof, unfeeling. Cats howled atop fences at two in the morning. We were a dog family. Dogs do their masters' bidding (supposedly), cats do not.

Susan and I wanted a kitten. For years we tried various schemes to persuade my mother—pleading, crying, pouting, demanding. Nothing worked. "We are not going to have a cat!" she said. Her tone of voice did not suggest negotiation.

Eventually, Winky died of old age. Later we moved to the farm. One cold, stormy evening with rain pelting down, I heard a faint squeaking sound outside. I opened the front door and went onto the porch. The sound was louder.

I opened the screen door. Sitting on the top step was a tiny, mud-soaked kitten, squeaking meows from its tiny mouth. It was drenched and pathetic looking.

I looked at it for a few minutes, tickled its chin, then dashed back inside. I snuck nonchalantly up to Susan's room and closed her door behind me.

"Susan, wait about two minutes, then come downstairs and meet me on the front porch," I said urgently.

She looked at me suspiciously. "What's this all about?"

"Don't ask questions. Just meet me on the porch," I said. "And be cool about it." Then I was gone. The conspiracy was afoot.

Two minutes later the front door opened. She poked her head out, checking in both directions to make sure it wasn't some kind of trick. I understood her caution. With siblings you can't be too careful.

"Don't worry. It's not a trick."

She came out onto the porch.

"Look," I said.

I opened the screen door and she came over. The kitten looked up at us in the fading light with eyes as big as saucers.

"A kitten!" she exclaimed. "Where did it come from?"

"I don't know. I heard this little squeaking and came out and found it."

"It's soaking wet."

"I know."

"Wait here," she said.

She disappeared inside and a few minutes later came

back out. She pulled out a bath towel from under her sweat shirt, picked up the kitten and started drying it off.

"It's shivering," she said.

I petted its tiny body and could feel it shaking.

"What are we going to do?" I asked. "We can't leave it outside in weather like this, but Mom and Dad will go nuts if they find it."

Susan thought for a moment while she cuddled the kitten next to her chest in the towel and dried its fur.

"Go back inside," she said, "and unlock the side door. And like you said to me, be cool about it. I'll wait a few minutes and come around from the outside."

"You'll get all wet. It's pouring."

"It's not far and it's mostly under the trees. I'll throw the towel over my head."

We lived in an old farmhouse. The side door was down half a flight of stairs from the main floor of the house and led directly from the outside into the basement so wood or coal could be hauled in without tracking through the house. I went through the den to the kitchen, hoping not to encounter my mother. I didn't. I opened the basement door, descended the half-flight of stairs and unlocked the side door. I peered out into the rainy darkness. After a bit Susan came running from under the trees. I opened the door and she slipped inside.

"Man, it's wet out there," she said. "This poor kitten would have drowned by morning."

We went into the basement and made a warm bed for the kitten. I emptied out a cardboard box full of old books, then found a batch of rags and old towels in the laundry room. Susan kept holding the kitten close to her body, trying to warm it up, cooing in its ear.

"We should feed it," she said. "It must be starving. Are you hungry, little sweetheart?" she said, stroking its head. "Hmm? Are you hungry?"

"What would be best to feed it?" I asked.

"Some warm milk."

"How are we going to do that without somebody noticing? We never drink warm milk."

"Was Mom in the kitchen when you came through?"

"No."

She thought for a minute. I could see her mind working.

"Here, hold the kitten for a while."

I took the kitten, wrapped in a dry towel now, into my arms like a baby. Susan disappeared into the front room of the basement. That's where all our boxes and junk were stored. I heard her moving things and rummaging around. In the light I looked closely at the kitten for the first time. Its fur was gray-brown with black tiger stripes, its little body scrawny. It had the weight of a tiny bag of feathers. But its face was sweet enough to make a Chicago gangster smile. The kitten wasn't nervous or fidgety. It settled into the warmth of my body as if it had been born there. I was already thinking about what we could name it.

Susan reappeared with a big grin on her face.

"Look what I found."

She held up an old hotplate with a frayed fabric-wrapped cord.

Putsy

"Problem solved," she said. "We can warm up the milk down here. You stay with the kitten. I'll go get some milk and a pan. If someone is in the kitchen it could take me a while so don't get worried."

Fifteen minutes later she returned with a small pan, a cereal bowl and a jar filled with milk.

"Mom was in the kitchen so I had to wait till she left. I brought some extra milk so we'd have a stock we can hide down here. There's a cooler in the front room we can store it in."

We plugged in the hotplate and warmed up some milk. We poured it into the cereal bowl and put the kitten down beside it. The kitten didn't know what to make of this and wandered off.

"Hey, little pussy cat, aren't you hungry?" Susan said. "Don't you want some nice warm milk, little putsy?" She picked up the kitten and put it down next to the bowl but it wandered off again. This time she picked it up and stuck its face straight into the bowl. It licked the milk off its whiskers and got the idea. The kitten was obviously starving. It lapped up the warm milk like it would never eat again.

"When are we going to tell Mom?" I asked. "She'll find the kitten as soon as she comes down the basement to do the laundry."

We didn't have much time to plot strategy. At that moment the basement door opened and Mom appeared at the top of the steps with a basket full of clothes. Susan and I scrambled to hide our crime. She tossed the towel over the top of the kitten and milk; I stood trying to block the hotplate and pan from view.

"What are you two doing down here?" Mom said as she walked down the stairs.

"Uh...uh...folding clothes?" Susan said.

"Folding clothes? At eight o'clock at night? That's a first."

The towel on the floor started moving around as if it were alive and we knew we were caught.

When Mom discovered what was under it she hit the roof.

"We will not have a cat in this house!" she pronounced.

Susan picked up the kitten.

"But, Mom, look at how cute it is. We don't have any pets. It's just a little kitten."

"You heard me."

"We can't just turn it outside in weather like this. It will die. It was all wet and shivering when we found it on the front steps. It's just a baby."

Mom hesitated a moment.

"You can keep it in the basement tonight, but tomorrow it goes. You'll have to find a home for it somewhere else."

Then Susan got smart.

"But it will be really good to have around. Remember all the trouble we've had with mice, how they get into things and you're always having to set traps? With a cat we would never have any mice. Every farmhouse needs a cat around. It would even keep rats away."

Rats! I shuddered.

Mom thought a minute.

"We'll talk about this in the morning. But I don't think I want a cat around."

Susan winked at me.

Putsy

The kitten stayed two days, then a week, then two weeks. I could see my mother softening. It was hard to look into the kitten's huge bright eyes and not be swayed. Dad didn't like the idea. He was a hunter. He wanted a hunting dog. But he would let Mom decide. We tried to convince him that having a cat didn't mean we couldn't also have a dog. We were getting greedy.

The decision was made by not being made. Mom didn't say that the kitten had to go so the kitten stayed. Susan and I were ecstatic.

Choosing a name became about as difficult as building the pyramids. The process seemed endless. We bandied possibilities about. Fluffy, Little Paws, Doris (the kitten was a girl), Whiskers, Tiger—monuments of originality. We made lists. We asked friends. We had family confabs. Nothing seemed right. In the meantime, while we were deciding on the perfect name, we called her "Putsy," so that we had something to call her. Putsy stuck.

As time went on, the inevitable happened. My mother, so resistant for so long to getting a cat, grew more attached to Putsy than she was to her own children.

As she grew from a kitten into a cat, we discovered that Putsy was a character. She was affectionate, ornery, unpredictable, and a hunter. She would appear proudly at the back steps and present us with a mouse like a child presenting an all-A report card. I loved to watch her hunt. She stalked like a lion. She possessed a balance, speed and grace of movement that were magical. She was like a dancer. And though she was small and rather delicate looking, she was fearless. We said among ourselves (though we'd never let our mother hear—such words weren't spoken in our house) that "Putsy didn't take shit from anything or anybody."

We had another dog for a while. It was a stray with a white and brown spotted coat that appeared one day and stuck around. Dad thought it looked like a good hunter, so we kept it. I remember the opening day of pheasant season. When the first shot rang out, the dog streaked back to the house like a speeding bullet, its tail literally between its legs. I'd never seen a dog so gun-shy. About this time Putsy had a litter of kittens in the basement. The dog (let's call him Spot—I don't remember his name because he didn't stick around too long) had the run of the first floor of the house. We were in the kitchen one evening doing dishes after dinner when we heard a terrible yelping sound and a cat's howl from the basement. We all blanched at once. "My God, the kittens!" Mom said. A split second later Spot careened up the basement stairs, smacked hard into the open door, and came to a stop panting in the kitchen. Blood ran from the claw marks on his nose. We ran downstairs to check Putsy and the kittens. She was lying on an old rug as serenely as if she'd just taken a long nap in the sunshine. There wasn't a mark on her and the four kittens frolicked on top of her.

Another time my friend Danny McAuliffe and I were playing baseball in the backyard, hitting each other grounders. Putsy sat on the side watching us, her head turning back and forth, back and forth, following the ball like a spectator at a tennis match. I noticed her creeping closer and closer, her eyes glued to the flight of the baseball.

I tossed up the ball, hit another grounder to Danny, and he threw it back to me. Putsy watched every movement of the ball as if it were a sparrow flitting from bush to bush. I tossed the ball up again and hit a hard grounder to Danny. Suddenly Putsy darted forward. She planted herself directly in the ball's path and crouched to attack it. I couldn't believe my eyes. The ball hit her flush on the nose. She leaped, exploded four feet into the air with a scream like a cartoon cat that's touched a ten-thousand-volt wire. She landed and shot off on a dead run. She streaked around the yard in a huge circle, then another and another, fast as lightning. She ran three big circles in a dead sprint, then abruptly pulled up and stopped. This electrified leap and sprint were heart-wrenching and utterly comical to watch. I was almost on the ground from laughter, but worried to death that she was hurt.

When she stopped I ran to where she sat in the grass. She looked up at me, panting hard but otherwise stock-still. Her nose was bleeding. Two drops of blood ran down from her tiny nostrils. I held her in my arms, petting her gently. She'd given us a fright, but she was fine. I wished that I had the whole scene on film for whenever I felt depressed and needed a good howl of laughter.

With Putsy, as with humans, there was a fine line between courage and stupidity. We once watched in prayer and horror from the kitchen window as a scene developed outside. But we weren't about to interfere. A skunk came ambling through the side yard, nosing about on its way from somewhere to somewhere. We had smelled it coming from upwind of us and hustled inside. Steve spotted the skunk crossing the dirt road in front of the house and it came into the yard. We all watched it from the window.

Suddenly Mom said: "Where's Putsy?"

We all looked at each other. No one knew.

"There she is!" I said.

She was crouched low in the grass, her gaze locked on the skunk fifty feet away.

"Oh, no," we said at once, anticipating the stench that would plague us for days.

Steve moved to run outside and try to get Putsy.

"Don't you dare!" Mom said. The skunk was a scant twenty feet from the house. We watched wide-eyed from the window like kids at a horror movie.

Skunks move with the disregard of lions. They don't possess the fear of a deer, a rabbit or an antelope because they are not hunted. A deer's senses are acute, its field of awareness huge. It picks up its head, always listening, smelling, watching. By comparison, the skunk seemed absentminded, nearsighted and careless. It ambled here, snooped there, without a worry in the world.

As the skunk moved, Putsy moved. At one point I was sure she was going to pounce. My heart tightened in my chest. I could almost see her muscles twitch in anticipation. But the moment passed and she moved farther down the yard. Then she made a wide loop around the skunk, climbed one of the big trees, and settled onto a wide branch about twelve feet above the ground. We all breathed a sigh of relief. She had finally abandoned her adventure and avoided this collision with disaster.

The skunk continued its amble toward the back

fields, stopping, starting, sniffing here and there (how it could smell anything was beyond me). We all slipped onto the screened-in back porch to get a better view. The skunk went past the side of the house where the lilacs grew and crossed under the tree where Putsy watched from her limb. When the skunk was ten feet beyond her, Putsy suddenly sprang from the branch like a flying squirrel. She sailed through the air, claws extended, and landed flush on the skunk's back. The skunk didn't know what hit it. They rolled and tussled until the skunk regained its feet and hightailed it for the field as fast as it could run. Putsy stood holding her ground, watching the intruder flee. We stood numb on the porch, waiting to be overwhelmed by a skunk smell ten times more powerful than any we'd smelled before.

We waited and waited. The odor never came. The skunk didn't spray! It must have been so shocked and surprised that its spray gland froze.

The opening day of pheasant season was a big event at the farm. My father's attorney friends and other hunting pals all gathered in what became an annual autumn ritual. They came early in the morning. My mother fixed coffee. The air was crisp. The corn stalks were brown and crackly in the fields.

One year I was standing out back as the men arrived. They came one or two to a car and wore heavy hunting boots. Their jackets and pants were field colors, tan or copper brown. The idea was to blend into the landscape, since anything shot at was flying in the air. Pheasant hunting wasn't as dangerous as deer hunting. Deer hunters blast away with rifles at any hint of movement in the forest. The dress of choice is day-glo orange or yellow, as if to say: "Don't shoot! I'm a human, not a deer." The last thing you want is to blend in, because a bullet might blend into your ribs.

As I watched the pheasant hunters gather this particular morning, there was a chill in the air. It was late October. I could see my breath. A brown stationwagon pulled into the driveway and parked. Art Taglia stepped out. Mr. Taglia owned an Italian restaurant in Flint. His son, Dennis, was a friend of my brother Tom. All the Taglias loved to hunt and they always had good hunting dogs. Mr. Taglia got out of the car, stretched, and greeted my father and the other men. He was just about to let his dog out of the back of the car when he saw Putsy. He stopped in mid-motion, closed the car back up and walked over to my dad.

"You know, John," he said, "you'd better put the cat inside before I let Duke out. He hates cats. In fact he's a real cat killer. He's killed something like sixteen cats over where we live." He said this with a mixture of remorse and bravado. I could tell he didn't like cats either. If anything, he was proud of Duke's exploits. To him hunting dogs were real animals. That they should kill useless cats was the natural order of things.

Duke was a Weimaraner, a big, powerful dog, maybe eighty pounds, with a beautiful gray-brown coat. Weimaraners are marvelous hunters with great noses for birds. It's thrilling to watch one work a field, freeze utterly motionless as it points a pheasant hiding in the deep grass, then finally flush the bird out.

Dad turned to me.

Putsy

"Why don't you put Putsy in the house, Pete."

Putsy was sitting by the big walnut tree near the back porch, calmly watching the activity.

"She'll be all right," I said.

Mr. Taglia looked at me like I was crazy.

"You really better put the cat inside, Pete. This dog will kill your cat," he said.

I looked over at Putsy.

"Don't worry, she'll be all right. She can take care of herself."

Mr. Taglia looked pleadingly at my father. He didn't want to be responsible for the death of his host's cat.

"You heard him, Art. He said not to worry. It's Pete's cat. You have certainly given him ample warning of the danger. If something happens, it's not your fault," Dad said.

"Okay," Mr. Taglia said, throwing his hands in the air. He walked back to his car to let Duke out.

This may seem like irresponsible behavior on my part, but I knew Putsy would be fine. Putsy was a survivor. She was sitting right next to the walnut tree and, if necessary, she could be up in its branches in the flash of an eye.

Mr. Taglia opened the back door of the stationwagon and Duke jumped out. All the hunters stood around to see what would happen. Duke was magnificent. The muscles rippled in his chest and shoulders. Just like a hunting dog, as soon as he hit the ground his nose was in the grass, sniffing everywhere. Putsy saw Duke before he saw her. Her response was immediate — the hair on her back stood straight up and her back arched high.

Duke rooted around like a bloodhound for a minute

or two. Everyone was still, watching. Putsy's back arched like the line of a bell curve. Duke stopped his sniffing, lifted his head and looked around. He spotted Putsy, thirty yards away. Their eyes locked on each other. Then, as if a starting gun had fired, Duke took off in a full sprint, straight at Putsy. My breath caught in my throat. A sudden fear shot through me.

It was over in a second. They met in a crash and Putsy let out a high scream. My heart nearly stopped. She flung herself straight into Duke's face, her claws out like the talons of a hawk. She dug her claws deep into Duke's snout. There was a whirl of motion and suddenly the big Weimaraner ran away, yelping, a sound of panic in its voice. It ran straight to the stationwagon and jumped back in.

A cheer and clapping erupted from the hunters. Mr. Taglia was dumbstruck.

"Well, I'll be..." he mumbled.

He ran over to check on Duke. Blood was running down his nose. Putsy stood regally by the walnut tree, all eight pounds of her. When Duke was finally coaxed back out of the car to go hunting, he skirted around the edge of the yard, far from where Putsy sat. After that day the legend of Putsy grew, and every year on the first day of hunting season, the hunters recalled the battle between Putsy and The Big Bad Cat Killer, Duke. Word got back to us that after that day, Duke never killed another cat.

Putsy was always pregnant. She was always having kittens. She must have had thirty-five or forty. We'd just finish giving away all the kittens in one litter when she would disappear for three or four days. She'd finally return looking haggard and bedraggled, and before long we'd notice her belly growing. It's a good thing that cats can't commit mortal sins with sexual transgressions the way humans can. Putsy would be shoveling coal in hell for a long time.

One summer morning I walked out the front door to get the newspaper. We were having a Michigan heat wave. At eight in the morning the temperature was in the high eighties. I came over the knoll leading down to the road and there was Putsy, lying down in the middle of the rise. She looked up at me lazily as I approached. I was surprised to find her resting there in the hot sun. Normally she'd be in the shade. I scratched her ears but couldn't shake the feeling that something looked unnatural, out of place. I noticed that her breathing was labored. Then I realized with a start that her back legs were lying at an impossible angle to the rest of her body. Her back was broken.

She'd been hit by a car. I could see in my mind what had happened. Unable to use her back legs, she had dragged herself out of the road with her front claws, through the rain ditch, and up the knoll until she could drag herself no farther. She must have been lying here for hours. I touched her fur and the bottom side of her coat was matted with dried blood.

I felt a flood of pain and panic. I wanted to take her in my arms and magically heal her. I wanted to take her pain away, and mine with it. I wanted her whole again. I ran into the house yelling for my mother. She was the only one still at home.

"Mom! Mom! Putsy's been hit by a car!"

We rushed out front and knelt down next to her. Putsy could barely hold up her head. Her eyes were hazy. My mother looked at her and tears started streaming down her face.

I ran in and called the vet. He said to get her in to him right away. He said to take a piece of stiff cardboard, slide it under her as gently as possible, place her in a large box and bring her to his office.

I ran out to the barn and found some boxes. We eased a flat piece of cardboard underneath her. She cried out in pain, but the cry was weak and I knew suddenly that very little life was left in her. We carefully picked up the cardboard, placed her in a box and put her in the back seat of the car.

I sat in the back seat with Putsy as Mom sped toward town. I looked down at her and thought of her antics and idiosyncrasies: jumping on the skunk, her run-in with Duke, all the kittens, the stormy night that Susan and I had found her as a kitten. Tears trickled down my cheeks. I softly stroked the fur on top of her head, trying to comfort her. I knew she liked that.

"You'll be okay, Putsy," I said. "The doctor will fix you. You'll be just fine."

She looked up into my eyes. She slowly blinked twice, and looked at me again. Then she closed her eyes, and as I stroked her head, she died.

We buried her back near the barn. I dug a hole in the dry ground, deep enough so other animals couldn't dig her up.

Putsy

We placed her gently in the bottom, wrapped in a white cloth. I fashioned a rough cross from two pieces of an oak limb and tied them together with heavy twine. I shoveled the dirt softly over her body and felt as though I was literally burying part of myself there in the dark, moist earth. That's where I would go one day, after I'd been run over by a car, shot by a careless hunter, or suffered some disease.

I made a neat mound, packed down the dirt with the shovel, and placed the wooden cross at the head of the grave. Then I sat down in the tall grass and stared into the distance for a long time.

The Little Ones

I always wanted a little brother or sister. My motivations were not noble. I hated being "the baby" of the family and I was sick of being knocked around by my older brothers. I wanted somebody that I could thump on now and then.

Hierarchy was a powerful force in my family. Status was assigned by age, by the birth order. There was a flip side to this coin, of course. My oldest brother had to forge trails through the virgin forests of childhood and growing up. With his position came responsibility, the need to be an example, and Johnny was the most serious of us children. I remember him with lines in his brow as a teenager. On the other hand, he had "station." He was consulted about things. He always got the best seat at the dinner table. In the car, the window seats automatically went to the oldest, in descending order of desirability. If either Mom or Dad weren't along, Johnny got the window in the front seat.

The Little Ones

Then Mike, then Tom got their choices. As the youngest, I always got the worst seat, the middle somewhere with my feet up on the hump in the floor. Driving up north with all eight of us and Winky crammed into the old Packard was a trial. There was a stretch around Midland (the home of Dow Chemical so the air always stunk) that was crawling with cops, a notorious speed trap. The law stated that a maximum of three people could ride in the front seat of a car. I was usually the fourth, stuffed into some crack so that all of us could fit in somewhere. But during that thirty-minute stretch around Midland, so that we wouldn't get a ticket for four in the front seat, I had to curl up and ride on the floor. It was me and the dog, together on the floor boards. This wasn't meant to be humiliating, but it was.

Two different times I nearly escaped my "Oh, you're the baby of the family" stigma. My mother got pregnant and her belly began to grow. I didn't know anything about the mechanics of the process, other than the fact that soon I would have a baby brother or sister. The stork must have visited while I was asleep at night. But both times she had miscarriages. The second time I was five or six. Mom came home from the hospital. She looked ashen. For several days a terrible hush fell over the house and I would see her crying.

    Even now, I sometimes think about my two little brothers or sisters (one of each is how I imagine them) who never made it to this world. What would they look like? Would they be funny? Would they be smart, or cranky, or like to sing? I think of all the games we would have played together, the sledding, the snowballs, the hide-and-seek and water-skiing. I think of what we would have learned and taught each other and experienced together. My family and my life were diminished by these accidents of fate, these early deaths of my two young siblings. They'd be in their sixties now.

Sin

The "Age of Reason" mystified me. Why did it suddenly begin at the age of seven, I wondered. What happened in the second grade that made me capable of committing sins? My seventh birthday approached like a black cloud in the distance. My soul had been pure and holy all my life. After my seventh birthday I could burn in hell. I wasn't at all sure that I could go through life without sinning. I would try, but....

The Age of Reason rules worked like this. You couldn't commit a sin before the age of seven, being too young to distinguish right from wrong. It was the theological equivalent, in temporal terms, of the insanity defense. This both insulted and thrilled me. On the one hand it said I was too young (read "dumb") to make rational decisions (despite the fact I could already add and subtract, though I couldn't do the multiplication tables). On the other hand, it gave me total freedom. I could do anything. In the eyes of the Church, I could do no wrong, though my parents didn't always agree. Mozart must have loved this Age of Reason rule. He could compose sonatas at age five but still had two years before he could commit a sin.

If you died before your seventh year and had been baptized (I was baptized at two weeks), your soul went directly to heaven. It was the straightest possible route — no stops in purgatory or limbo — because you'd never been capable of committing a sin. Baptism was the key. Baptism was the first of the Seven Sacraments. It cleansed your soul. It erased the black stain of Adam and Eve's original sin that blights us all at birth (except for the Virgin Mary). Baptism conferred on the soul a state of pure grace, a God-like purity — until the age of seven. Then everything changed.

I decided that if I were to die young, I wanted to go just before I turned seven. That would be ideal. I'd go straight to heaven. A month or two before my birthday would be perfect. That way I'd get to enjoy all of my pre-Age of Reason grace years. All that fun and mischief with no threat of punishment (other than from my parents, of course, but I was clever enough to deal with them). After reflecting, I decided that a few months before my birthday was too far in advance. Since my birthday fell on January 13th, if I died two months beforehand I'd miss Christmas. Uncle George's potato chips would be coming and I wanted a new Wyatt Earp pistol and holster for Christmas, which I mentioned in my prayers every night. I wanted at least a little time to enjoy it. So I started to pray that I'd die on January 10th. That way I'd live through the holidays, but I'd miss the Age

Sin

of Reason—the Age of Sin and Probable Burning.

Dying on January 10th and getting a Wyatt Earp pistol for Christmas seemed like perfectly appropriate subjects for prayer. I prayed for dozens of things—that Diane Ferris would stop kissing me on the playground, for instance. She'd hide somewhere and while I was playing tag, my eyes intent on whoever was "It," she'd sneak up and plant a big kiss on my cheek. I jumped like I'd been bitten by a rattlesnake. All the girls would laugh. The boys would point and shout: "Petie loves Diane! Petie loves Diane!" "I do not!" I'd yell back and chase them till I could shove somebody. That was the requisite show of prowess. Then we would go on with our game. About three years later I prayed that Sally Jackson would kiss me on the playground. We constantly sent love notes back and forth in class. "See you near the flagpole at recess. I love you," I'd write. When Sister William wrote something on the blackboard (which was always green even though they called it black), I'd fold the note and pass it to Tommy Jacobs who'd pass it to Mary Satterlee who'd pass it to Sally. "I love you more," she'd write back. This went on for weeks. "Dear God, please let me marry Sally when we grow up," I'd pray at night. A year later I prayed that I'd marry Connie Stevens from "Hawaiian Eye" on T.V. I prayed that the Detroit Tigers would win the pennant (fat chance). I said rosaries that my brother, Steve, would break his foot so I could hit him for a change and he wouldn't be able to catch me.

Steve threw terrible temper tantrums. He was almost three years past the Age of Reason and it hadn't done a thing for his rationality. He yelled and screamed and his face turned bright red. Everyone said this was because of his red hair. Redheads had terrible tempers. Steve proved the rule in spades, hearts and diamonds.

As luck would have it, my seventh birthday came and went and I didn't die. Some prayers get answered and some don't. I passed into the Age of Reason and my soul passed from purity to peril. One by one my list of "nevers" passed away. I would never commit a sin, I told myself. I did. I would absolutely never commit a mortal sin, one of those transgressions for which you can burn in hell. I did that too, eventually. Most of my mortal sins were sexual in nature. The Catholic Church smiles less on sex than on superstition, especially sex before marriage. I had a while to wait. I couldn't.

My early mortal sins were self-inflicted. Masturbation, adults and textbooks would call it. We called it "playing with yourself," "jacking off," "slamming the salami," "whacking it." For me it was an intensely private, ecstatic, condemning act. I wouldn't begin with the idea of completion, of proceeding on to that magic moment of eruption. I always intended to stop short, before I crossed over from venial to mortal sin. I could almost never stop. The first wave of pleasure would wash toward me and a moment later I would be lost in its power, unable, unwilling to turn back. Immediately afterward I would sink into a chasm of guilt and shame. How could I be so weak, so detestable. Each time I committed this act I pushed the spear deeper into Christ's side as he hung suffering on the cross.

I remember the first time I masturbated. I was twelve years old. We had just moved to the farm. One afternoon everyone was gone and I was all alone in our big old house. I went to my parents' bedroom and opened my mother's dresser drawer. The articles of clothing inside were so strangely different from boys'. Underpants with no overlap opening in the front; brassieres; a contraption with four strange button-like clips suspended from what I took to be a waistband. This one intrigued me. I later discovered it was called a garter belt and held up nylon stockings. The material was strong but satiny and very smooth.

    I took this from the drawer and went down the hallway to the bathroom. I locked the bathroom door. That way no one could come home without my knowing and surprise me doing something I knew must be forbidden. I took all my clothes off. I clipped the garter belt around my chest to see if it was some kind of brassiere. Maybe it held up a woman's underpants. That didn't seem right. I put it around my waist, orienting it in different directions. I was too small to see what it looked like in the mirror. I put the toilet seat cover down and stood on top of the toilet so I could see better. I slid the garter belt sideways until one of the clips hung down directly in front over my penis. I pulled the clip between my legs and hooked it to the waistband in back. The strong, satiny material pulled tight over my small boy's erection. As I stood on top of the toilet with this strange garment around my waist, I instinctively rubbed my penis through the satiny cloth. Gradually, some unknown feeling began to gather there. I kept rubbing and after a few minutes an exquisite sensation rippled through my whole body, focused just beneath my fingers. I felt a sudden shudder. My knees went weak and I nearly fell off my perch.

A small circle of liquid spotted the material of the garter belt.

I stepped raggedly from atop the toilet seat and sat breathless on the bathroom floor, my back against the wall. I was confused and startled, amazed. I had stumbled onto some precious emerald of feeling so outside my range of experience that I had no idea what to think.

After a while I gathered myself. I put my clothes back on and rinsed the spot from the garter belt. No one was home yet. I turned on the iron, dried the wet material with the heat, and slipped the garter belt back inside the drawer where I had found it.

Over the coming weeks I grew addicted to this feeling. I discovered that I could lie on my stomach in bed, rub myself back and forth on the sheets and the sensation would come. Everyday after school I'd come home and disappear into my room. I'd lie face down on the bed and rub my erection rhythmically, frantically against the sheet. Soon, with the friction and rubbing, the catharsis approached. I tightened and this wave, so original and perfect, so full of ecstasy, swept over me and the world disappeared. Sometimes I'd do it again before going to sleep, after I had said my prayers and tucked myself in. The feeling was exquisite and joyful, indescribable. At night it was like drinking warm milk before bedtime. I'd fall asleep feeling warm and secure inside.

Then I discovered something...I was committing mortal sins!

I can't remember how I found this out. I had discovered a jewel in my existence and it was ripped away from me. I had vowed never in my life to commit a mortal sin. I realized that I'd been doing just that for months. I rationalized that I actually hadn't yet committed a mortal sin because I hadn't known—ignorance of the law is an excuse. But now I knew. I was no longer ignorant. I became very frightened. How could I not do this? This was an act I loved, more than leaping to snatch a high drive deep in center field. How could I control the power of my desire and instinct? Who did this hurt?

The answer, according to the Church, was that it hurt Jesus. It drove the nails further into his palms and pushed the sharp thorns hard into his forehead. It also hurt me. Masturbating made me morally degenerate, I was told. It made me corrupt and despicable—a sinner. God wouldn't love little boys who did such a hateful act. It would make me lose my soul. If I committed a mortal sin and died before I got to confession, I would go to hell. I would burn—BURN!!--for all eternity. This seemed like a heavy price for a few moments of pleasure. I started having nightmares about hell, about the burning. I hadn't had one in years. "But God gave me these feelings," I said to myself in confusion. "We're taught that our bodies are made in the image and likeness of God. How can something God created be so evil? Why would He do that?" "To test our love for Him," the priest told me. This seemed cruel to me, like dangling food in front of starving people, but telling them it was a sin to eat.

I had crossed into the Age of Reason, that epoch filled with perils and consequence. I discovered my weaknesses. Reaching the Age of Reason was like rounding a bend on a beautiful mountain trail and suddenly facing a treacherous precipice. The trail became perilous and steep, bordered

Wild Blueberries

by dragons and plunges into canyons of fire. I wasn't wild about this Age of Reason and mortal sin. Eternity is a long time to burn.

TRIBES

Tribalism fascinates me. It frustrates and frightens me. I wonder why we humans gravitate so relentlessly toward paradigms of "Us" and "Them." We divide along lines of race and religion. If no natural division exists there, we simply traverse until we locate (or create) other categories to divide us—class, education, politics, accent, gender, clan, country, neighborhood, the foods we like, the cars we drive, the elongation of our vowels, the curl or straightness of our hair, job description, tattoos or no, whether we are Yankees, Dodgers, or Red Sox fans. Within large, relatively homogeneous groups we move inward to smaller and smaller circles until we clarify what and who we are by contrast with what and who we are not. We search divisions out, it seems, with the devotion and tenacity of old prospectors seeking gold in the dry, rocky hills of the Nevada desert. We find our precious differences, then build our walls with bricks of hate.

WILD BLUEBERRIES

I first encountered this tribal Us and Them—in a guise of which I was conscious—in catechism class. We, as Catholics, were The Chosen Ones, God's special children. We alone could enter the gates of heaven when we died and bask for all eternity in the Holy Trinity's sacred light (and have endless supplies of Oreo cookies, blueberry pies, and frozen lemon custard, I presumed, since in heaven you were always happy and never sad). We could get into heaven because we were baptized into the One True Faith.

Baptism was the first of the seven sacraments and our key into the Kingdom. If you were not baptized a Catholic you could not get into heaven. Simple as that. All those other poor bastards (not the nun's words, precisely, but that was the general drift), all the unbaptized and bereft, the Methodists and Jews, the Lutherans, Presbyterians and Buddhists, the Muslims, Baptists and Hindus, would have to make do with limbo (the afterlife's version of vacationing at Lake of the Ozarks—pleasant enough, for a time, but you still have mosquitoes, flies and chiggers to deal with), or go straight to hell—the more likely result because they wouldn't have the grace of God to help keep them on the straight and narrow.

This whole concept of us Catholics as the chosen few made me uneasy and gave me pause. It seemed to say that Abraham Lincoln, for instance, could not get into heaven. Honest Abe! He had sacrificed. He'd learned to read by the light of a candle. He had freed the slaves, given his life, and saved the country. But I'd never heard that he was a Catholic (and Sister Angelica surely would have touted such a sterling example of tribal celebrity—Bing Crosby was a Catholic, after all, and we all knew that). It meant that Gandhi could not go to heaven. Or the Dalai Lama. Or some sweet child who grew up in the African bush and had never even HEARD of Catholics. If God was so good, so all-knowing, loving and merciful, how could this be possible? It made no sense to my child's mind.

The tribal hatred with the Russians in the 1950s was like a force of nature. We were taught in school that "The Reds," "The Commies," were evil and Godless. Nikita Kruschev pounded his shoe and shouted "We will bury you!" We watched pictures of mushroom clouds on the black and white television screen (there was no color in those days), heard talk of A-bombs and H-bombs, and dove under our classroom desks during drills for when The Bomb came (I remember whacking my head on several occasions). My father talked to a man about digging a bomb shelter in our backyard. It would be dug near the big elm tree by the back fence and be made of heavy steel with thick concrete walls. I imagined it would be an awful place, dark and dank and intolerably cold. What if we had to go there in the wintertime? I waited each day for the man to return and start digging, but he never came. I don't know if the bomb shelter was too expensive, life just got too busy, or if my parents decided that if someday it were needed, it would be too late anyway.

Flushing was a small town in those days, with a two-block-long downtown and none of the "subdivisions" that later began to dot the outskirts of every hamlet and village in America, wiping out the farmland. There were no suburbs or malls. Malls were the invention and sociological abomination of a later time. Small downtowns were still alive and vital in the 1950s.

In 1957 Flushing was all white. There was not a single black child in school nor a black family in town, at least not that I knew of. I had seen black people before because Flint, the big city nearby where Dad worked and which was later immortalized by Michael Moore in "Roger and Me," had lots of black people, many of whom worked in the car factories. But I had never met or talked to a black person. Flint was a long way away, probably ten miles, and we seldom went there except to be tortured by the dentist or maybe go Christmas shopping. But for my eighth birthday my parents gave me a membership to the Flint YMCA. This membership had nothing to do with the Christian element of the YMCA and everything to do with the swimming pool. In truth it had little to do with the swimming aspect of the pool and everything to do with the diving board. Having spent most summers in my life at Platte Lake, I could swim at a young age and was like "a fish" around the water. "Why, that boy swims just like a fish," people said to my mother when I was little.

But for some reason, I wanted to dive. Had I already seen the Acapulco cliff divers immortalized on Wide World of Sports? That came later, I think. I had probably seen Johnny Weissmuller dive into the gorge of some African river to escape an evil big game hunter in a Tarzan movie. But at some point I must have rhapsodized aloud about diving—so my parents gave me this YMCA membership because kids could learn to dive there.

On Saturday mornings Dad dropped me at the Y

on the way to his office and picked me up about three hours later. I was scared to go in at first. The building was old and imposing, made of dark red brick, and I didn't know a soul. Looking at it the first time, I thought I'd get swallowed up inside. I'd get lost and never find my way out. But I quickly grew comfortable. There were only four or five kids in the diving class, and by being in the class we were automatically on the "YMCA Diving Team" (not that that turned out to mean much—we never had a competition against anybody). We started out by diving off the side of the pool (even Dumbo the Elephant could do that), then gradually advanced to the diving board. We learned the swan dive (which Johnny Weissmuller did beautifully), the jackknife, a reverse jackknife, and a modified swan dive with a half twist. It was great. I loved it. Diving was like being a bird, soaring, floating through the air with a perfect grace, even if only for moments.

Some of the kids couldn't master the swan dive, which always seemed the easiest to me. They couldn't make it all the way through the curve to enter the water vertically. They would flatten out in the air, stay horizontal and suddenly a loud CLAP would echo through the pool house—another "bellysmacker." They would haul themselves slowly up the ladder from the pool, grimacing, and unfurl to expose their belly and chest, red as a cooked lobster.

My personal nightmare was the somersault. No matter how I tried or practiced, I could never get the timing down. I would bounce upward from the diving board, go into a tuck, and become totally disoriented as I spun in the air. I would hit the water SMACK on my back, or my face, or my side. SMACK, SMACK, SMACK! And I too would crawl out of the pool, red like the others and wanting to howl.

But my favorite thing about diving at the YMCA became Billy Johnson. Billy was a Negro boy from Flint (the term "African-American" had not been coined in 1957, nor was "black" yet a part of the lexicon) who became my buddy in diving class. Billy and I were shy of each other at first. We were, after all, from a whole menagerie of different tribes, separated—if we had chosen difference as our focus—by race, religion, economic class, parental education, public school versus Catholic school, city versus small town. But we didn't give much thought to either our differences or our commonalities. We were simply two young boys who grew to love diving together, and we liked each other. Billy was smart and funny and inventive. He had more depth and substance than other kids I knew, and sometimes when we talked, I felt he imparted some of that depth to me. We were both skinny, but he was stronger than me and did great somersaults (though I did a better swan dive). We created all manner of games to play in the pool after class and when we practiced our diving. We took turns bringing a deck of cards and played "Fish" together till Dad picked me up.

Billy's most distinctive physical characteristic was not the color of his skin. It was his scars. If you met him dressed he looked completely normal. But in his bathing suit you saw that nearly his entire torso, upper arms, and the tops of his thighs were thickly scarred with a recurring pattern that looked like scalloped seashells about the size of a nickel. In the dressing room one day not long after we'd met, I asked him what had happened to his skin. When he was little one of his uncles had slipped on the kitchen floor and accidentally knocked a cauldron of boiling water off the stove, which splashed all over Billy. The burns were so bad that for a while everyone thought he would die. Eventually he healed, but his body was left with skin like scalloped seashells.

I still think of Billy Johnson sometimes. We lived a long way from each other and lost contact after diving class. Kids didn't talk on the telephone in those days and computer chat rooms did not exist. I have wondered over the years where he might be, what his life is like, whether he is still alive. I can see even now the lively smile on his face or his brow knotted in serious thought as he spoke. Billy was the first person of another race, of his particular tribe, that I ever met. I suspect that my parents had a purpose in giving me that YMCA membership for my eighth birthday beyond just teaching me to dive. I think they wanted me to step outside the walls of our own tribe and encounter, early on, the humanity that existed beyond, before the walls of stereotype, division, and closed-mindedness could grow too high and harden.

Billy was not a Catholic, but I think that if he died, he surely would have gone to heaven.

WILD BLUEBERRIES

Blueberries are magic to me. Left alone on a desert island with one meal to eat before I died, I would want blueberries. They are more than taste and texture to me. They are evocation. They awaken in me a sense of rare beauty, a sense of joy, nostalgia and exultation.

I don't know how or why this started. When I was a child our birthdays were special events. We were excused from all our chores and duties for the day. We didn't even have to do dishes. We could request our favorite meal for dinner and my mother would fix it, along with a birthday cake with candles for dessert. I always asked for blueberry pie instead of a cake. Everyone thought this was crazy. But my mother would bake the pie and after dinner she would turn off the lights, bring in my pie glowing with candles, and I felt like royalty.

Sometimes up North we'd pick fresh fruit in the

summertime — strawberries, cherries, Elberta peaches, blueberries. The blueberries were my favorite. Two handfuls went into my mouth for every handful into the bucket. I'd eat them on cereal, in a bowl with milk, with sliced peaches, or right out of the big ceramic bowl in the refrigerator. I ate blueberries the way most kids eat popcorn and candy.

When I was in my mid-twenties a friend and I drove across the country from California to visit my parents at the cottage in Northern Michigan. As a treat my mother bought two quarts of fresh-picked local blueberries. I entered into the first reaches of heaven. I hadn't had quarts of blueberries for years. In California blueberries were sold by the thimbleful at the cost of sapphires. The crop that year was spectacular. The berries were plump, crisp, sweet and as big as marbles. By nightfall the two quarts were gone. I was trying to be polite, which was the only reason they lasted that long. The next day as my friend, Kitty, and I left for the grocery store, my mother suggested that I pick up two more quarts. We could make a pie. Kitty and I ended up at Stone's Farm Market out on the road past Beulah. Two hours later we walked into the cottage, not with two quarts, but with ten pounds of blueberries. My mother's jaw dropped.

"What in the world will we do with all those?" she asked, alarmed. My mother was a bride of the Depression. The idea of waste unsettled her. I wasn't sure myself what we'd do with ten pounds of blueberries, but I figured we'd manage something. Two pies, four days and countless bowls and handfuls later, they were all gone. I went to buy more — and came back with another ten pounds.

Memory and wonder mix with the taste of blueberries

in my mind. They transport me to moments of power and beauty in my life: to the tiny blueberry farm (two acres at most) hidden deep in the woods down a gravel road near Platte Lake where I picked the small round berries alone or with my father. Going to that blueberry farm in the woods in late summer or early autumn is a rite of visitation for me, even now. I return there as pilgrims return to Mecca or Lourdes, to renew connections in my spirit and psyche.

Wild Blueberries

Once I was walking in the virgin hills of Northern Sweden. It was late June, the summer solstice. Darkness fell at midnight and two hours later it was light again. Nature's presence was powerful and unfolding. Moose roamed the forests. I walked over a hillock and stumbled onto a meadow of wild blueberries. I had never seen wild blueberries. I didn't know somehow that wild blueberries existed. I was struck with wonder, as if I had seen God. The moment is frozen in my memory. I stayed in that meadow the entire afternoon, lolling in the sunshine, feasting on the wild berries like a bear in summer. I felt joined to nature and history, joined to the wild animals and ancient humans who had fed on those berries over the course of centuries. It struck me that, of course, blueberries were wild before they were domesticated, that most things were wild before becoming domesticated: apples, strawberries, rhubarb, cats, potatoes, human beings. Sometimes the memory of our species is short.

Years later I was trekking in the high Andes of Peru, over sections of the ancient Inca Trail. The power and vistas of those sharp-cut mountains were humbling, titanic. The Andes are the second highest range in the world. Only the Himalayas rise higher. We were walking far above the treeline, at nearly 14,000 feet. Nearby the immense presence of Mt. Salcantay rose toward the heavens. Its snowcapped 20,574-foot peak glistened in the sunlight.

The air was remarkably thin. I'd advance a hundred feet up the steep trail and have to stop, my lungs heaving for air. The vegetation was mostly high grasses, dotted with the color flecks of wild flowers. As I labored upward I became gradually aware of another plant growing here and there on the mountainside. It was a determined-looking little bush, about eighteen inches tall, with thin, tough branches and small leaves. Only after I had huffed past twenty or thirty did I become aware of them. Something about these plants drew me. Finally I knelt down and looked at one closely. In amongst the leaves I discovered a small, dark berry. I picked one and examined it. A sudden feeling like love swept over me. I was holding a blueberry. An Andean wild mountain blueberry. I knelt there, in awe but somehow unsurprised that here, in these majestic mountains that moved me more than any place I'd been on earth, I would encounter these old friends. My emotions are close at hand in such places. The blueberry bushes ignited a deep sense of joy in me. They seemed like people, like cousins, like the spirits of tiny guardian angels that traveled the world with me. I ate a few of the berries. They weren't as juicy as lowland berries, but were at once sweet and tart. A broad smile crossed my face. I couldn't believe it—blueberries, in this place, this place so near to God.

  That evening I sat atop a mountain aerie watching Salcantay. The spot where I sat was aptly named. It is called "Phuyupatamarca" by the Quechua Indians of these mountains, "Site on the Clouds." I could see for miles and miles in every direction. At the base of the escarpment below me was an Inca holy place. There was a line of ritual baths for cleansing the spirit, mind and body, and a long, beautiful "huaca" nearby, a sacred rock in which the Incas believed the spirits of the earth live.

  I couldn't take my eyes off the mountain. Salcantay

rose into the sky with awesome, silent power. As I sat there I realized suddenly that it was Father's Day. I sat alone and thought of my father, Big John, who had died ten months before. I thought of the blueberries I'd encountered on the mountain that afternoon and remembered the last time he and I had picked blueberries together at Platte Lake. It was autumn. The trees were turning color. I was surprised to find berries still on the bushes. We climbed into Dad's knock-around car, the old green Ford Fairlane with the fenders rusted out. We turned off the main road by the Cherry Bowl Drive-In, then onto a gravel road through the oak and maple forests, and finally onto the dirt track that led to the blueberry farm.

 Before we arrived at the small house in the maple trees Dad stopped the car. I didn't know why but figured there was some good reason. He got out, so I did too. He surveyed the landscape. He loved this country. He'd rather be here in Northern Michigan than anywhere in the world. After a moment he walked around and opened the trunk. He unwrapped something from a blanket next to the spare tire and pulled out a bottle of whiskey. He took a slug from it and offered the bottle to me.

 "Want a swig?" he said with a smile, his good-natured tone cut with an edge of defiance.

 "No thanks," I said.

 My head started spinning. I was devastated. I wanted to bolt, to run away through the trees. Years of anguish, denial and conflict rushed into me as if pouring through a sluice gate. He was an alcoholic, though none of us ever breathed the word. I thought he hadn't had a drink for seven years. When he was sober he was delightful. When he drank he could be despicable and consumed by his rage. I hated him then. The drinking hadn't seemed to hurt his work much over the years, but it had hurt us—me, his wife, his whole family, and himself. He was a diabetic. Now he had cancer. The drink had almost killed him before. Would it finish off the job now? I immediately feared for my mother. Not physically, but emotionally, psychologically. I wanted to grab the bottle and smash it on a rock. But I didn't. I couldn't. I thought it would create an impassable chasm between us. And maybe, if I were in his shoes, facing his diseases, his cancer, I would want a drink too.

He put the bottle back in the trunk. We got into the car and drove to the farmhouse. We had a good time the rest of the day. He left the bottle in the trunk. We both loved being in the blueberry patch, searching among the green leaves for the sparse clumps of berries. We filled the better part of two plastic buckets and I ate half-again as much while I picked. The air was clear and moist. The sky changed. Clouds rode across the sun on the wind. The breeze rose and fell. It was one of these early autumn days, as the season slips from summer toward winter, that fills me with joy and stillness. No one was home at the farm. It ran on the honor system. Dad weighed out the blueberries on the old scale in the shed and left the money on the table, along with some extra for what we'd eaten. We drove home. Mom and I made a blueberry pie and I ate my cereal in the mornings with a mound of blueberries on top. I didn't see the bottle again that trip.

Sunset turned Salcantay pink, then mauve with

its changing light. I looked into the silent power of the mountain. I felt my dead father's presence beside me. I felt his presence all around me in the air.

"I love you, Dad," I said out loud, and tears trailed down my cheek.

After a while I walked down to the campsite. At dinner with the rest of the expedition, I raised a toast to all our fathers on this Father's Day, to those alive and dead, and to the fathers there among us. We shared a moment of silent reflection. Then we talked again of our walk up the mountainside.

"Could you believe those wild blueberries?" I said.

Holy Communion

We went to mass every morning in grade school. That was the rule. Those were the days of the Latin mass, when the priest still faced away from the congregation, looking toward the crucifix of the dying Christ on the back wall, and you had to fast before receiving Holy Communion. The Church's fasting laws said that if you wanted to go to Communion at the morning mass you couldn't eat anything after twelve midnight. The body needed to cleanse itself and be purified to receive the Body of Christ. In other words, no breakfast. I loved breakfast. It was my favorite meal. This created a dilemma for me — sustenance of my body or my soul, selfishness or sacrifice, food or everlasting life.

Going to Communion was a many-edged sword. It was social performance — you rose before the whole congregation, marched to the altar and displayed your piety and state of grace to everyone. It was a way to gain approval

Holy Communion

from the nuns. They definitely noticed who did and did not go to Communion (you had to be careful not to go too often, though, or the other kids would shun you as a show-off and a brown-nose). But fasting and going to Communion also gave me a feeling of strength and self-discipline, of triumph over the weakness of being human. And now and then I even experienced the original intent—a spiritual joining with Christ, a sense of truly receiving Him into my body and soul.

So on those mornings when I decided to fast and go to Holy Communion, Mom packed some little breakfast (note the derivation of the word: breakfast—the breaking of the fast). An orange or banana and toast or a donut in a brown paper bag. I'd eat it after mass and be starving by lunchtime. To strike some balance between holiness, sustenance and social acceptability, most of us went to Communion a couple of times a week.

In the seventh or eighth grade a drastic change occurred. The Catholic Church altered the fasting rules. They wanted to make it easier for the faithful to go to Communion. Suddenly we only had to fast for an hour beforehand, instead of from midnight onward. This meant that we could get up in the morning, eat a big breakfast and still go to Communion. The effect at mass was dramatic. Now, instead of maybe a third of the students going to Communion on any given day, everyone went, every day. There was no reason not to. The pews emptied totally, one by one, starting at the front of the church and moving backward. A big line formed down the middle aisle. The cost to the parish for Communion wafers must have skyrocketed.

I didn't like this change. It cheapened Communion in my mind. It removed the sacrifice and choice. Communion became prescribed and automatic instead of special. The change also created a major problem. There was one reason not to go to Communion—mortal sin. Not being in the state of grace. If you'd committed venial sins you could still receive Holy Communion. Sins like lying or stealing a popsicle from the drugstore or smacking your brother when he wasn't looking. Even impure thoughts. These didn't totally blacken the soul, but were merely black spots on the soul's white grace. I imagined that the soul with venial sins looked like the coat of a Holstein cow. But mortal sins were different. It was forbidden, utterly unthinkable, to go to Communion and receive the Body of Christ inside if you had committed a mortal sin. It was the ultimate desecration. If such a thing as a hierarchy of mortal sins existed, a worst of the worst, a black beyond blackness that would make the flames in hell burn hotter, this would be it. If you committed a mortal sin, you had to go to confession before going to Communion again—and pray you didn't die before you got to the confessional.

With the new fasting rules, whenever one of us didn't go to Communion it could mean only one thing—we had committed a mortal sin. Which in turn could mean only one thing—we had whacked it. There weren't many mortal sins available for twelve- or thirteen-year-olds to commit. Willfully missing church on Sunday was one. But what else? "Coveting your neighbor's wife," whatever that was? Murder? Not hardly. There was only masturbation, jacking off. And the moment I stayed in my pew and didn't go to

Holy Communion

Communion, the whole school knew I'd done it. This was a horrible, shameful feeling. It was like wearing a scarlet letter, like being paraded naked around the playground with my penis in my hand. Whenever one of the seventh or eighth grade boys hung back in their pew, their eyes riveted downward in shame, we all knew—they'd whacked it the day before. No one ever said anything, but everyone knew. Now and then one or two of the girls didn't go to Communion either. I always assumed they felt ill or had forgotten and eaten something during the hour before Communion (the same excuses we boys lamely attempted). I never imagined that maybe girls masturbated too. I didn't know they could. They didn't have a pecker to do it with. I both pitied and envied them this fact. Pitied them because a pecker gave rise to these exquisite sensations. But I envied them because they didn't carry around the curse of this instrument of sin and damnation. Girls weren't driven by lust the way boys were. I figured girls had a better chance of getting to heaven because they didn't possess a cock inside their panties. Only later did I learn more about girls' anatomy and sexual appetites, and that inside their panties they possess a whole array of instruments of energy, lust and power.

Holy Communion and the Catholic mass contained a great mystery. Simple bread and wine were changed into the Body and Blood of Christ. This was not presented as symbolic ritual. It was presented as literal fact. It was a miracle. The small bread wafer became literally the Body of Christ, which we received on our tongues. This wafer, the host, was sacred. It was the flesh of Christ Himself. Only the priest could touch it because his hands were specially consecrated. The Eucharist was carried in a golden chalice-like ciborium and housed in a locked golden tabernacle next to a flame that always burned because the Body of Christ was there. I, of course, accepted all this as gospel truth.

My First Communion was a grand event, as it was every year. I was seven years old (yes, First Communion coincides with the Age of Reason). We studied the catechism for weeks beforehand. We went to confession for the first time. "Bless me, Father, for I have sinned. This is my first confession."

At our First Communion all of us, both boys and girls, were dressed completely in white, head to toe, to signify the purity of our young souls and the sacred purity of Christ. We were like little angels without the wings. White shirt, white pants, white socks, white belt. We even wore white ties. I had never seen a white tie before.

The ceremony was at a Sunday morning high mass, complete with the choir singing and tall candles. When the moment for Communion arrived, we filed out of our pews before the rest of the congregation, approached the Communion rail and knelt down. There were about thirty-five of us, the whole second grade class except for Jimmy Simpson, who had failed second grade the year before and received his First Communion then.

I was filled with fear and anticipation. My hands were sweating and I could barely breathe. My heart pounded in my chest. Father Jacobs approached from the right, moving slowly along the Communion rail, placing the round white

HOLY COMMUNION

host on my classmates' tongues one by one.

Suddenly it was my turn. My hands were folded piously in front of my chest. I put my head back, opened my mouth and stuck out my tongue. Father Jacobs softly placed the host on my tongue. It was light as a robin's feather. I could barely feel it.

For a few seconds I didn't close my mouth. The Body, the very flesh of Christ, rested on my tongue. I felt a sense of wonder, yet a wave of revulsion swept over me. I felt vaguely cannibalistic. I closed my mouth and almost gagged. The host was indescribably dry. It stuck to the roof of my mouth like adhesive paper and sucked up all the moisture. It tasted like white paste. Walking back to my pew, my head bowed and hands folded like a pious Saint Peter, I frantically worked my tongue against the roof of my mouth, trying to scrape loose the host that was stuck there like a postage stamp. Gradually it came away in small pieces.

Holy Communion and such "miracles" affect one's thinking. I grew up with lots of miracles: the Assumption, when the Blessed Virgin Mary was raised bodily into the heavens to take her place with the Trinity; the loaves and fishes, when Christ fed thousands from a few small morsels of bread and fish; the raising of Lazarus from the dead; the Immaculate Conception. I believed in the literal truth of these events. Each time I assisted the priest as an altar boy at mass, I believed that the small round wafers and red wine truly became the Body and Blood of Christ as the priest raised them heavenward, spoke the special prayers, and I rang the altar bells in celebration.

After enough years of such exposure, belief in

miracles creates a certain bent in the mind, like the windswept curve of trees near the ocean. Miracles beget optimism, an unconscious faith that possibility exists in the universe. The problems begin when these beliefs and the child encounter the modern world and scientific method. Empiricism and Holy Communion don't ride comfortably in the same cart. One or the other gets jolted out. The child studies the laws of physics: Energy is neither created nor destroyed. But what about the loaves and fishes? The doctrines of the modern god, science, are hammered into the mind and conflicts arise. I recall my confusion. The questions. The terror and discomfort. If I didn't believe in the Transfiguration of Christ would I burn forever in hell? But if I believed in the Assumption and the Virgin Birth would I burn in the hell of ignorance? I searched for common ground, for shades of gray. I usually found fields of black and white, irreconcilable differences. "The test of a first-rate intelligence is the ability to hold two opposed ideas in the mind at the same time, and still retain the ability to function," F. Scott Fitzgerald wrote. I flunked the test.

The Knothole

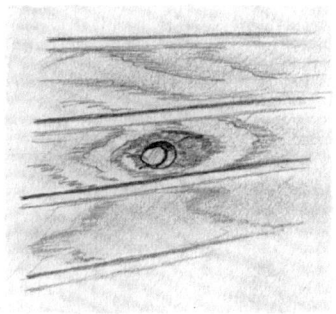

I have little memory of my oldest brothers while I was growing up. Johnny was a dozen years older than me, Mike nine, and Tom six or seven. When I was seven years old and facing the Age of Sin and Reason, Johnny was already away at college.

My picture of him wasn't rounded and complete. In my mind he was a basketball player. He played starting forward on Flushing High's championship basketball team. The center and the other forward were the Porn twins, Jim and Jack. That really was their last name. What a front line: two Porns and a Damm—from a town called Flushing. The Porns were 6'4" and 6'8". Johnny was 6'4". In 1955 that made a very tall high school basketball team.

This team held the town's emotions in a vice grip. They played in a tiny, crackerbox gym that on game nights sweltered and rocked with noise. Jim Porn launched jump shots from behind his head with his feet pulled up behind him, and Johnny sank graceful hook shots from the right side.

I remember my brothers Mike and Tom more clearly than I remember Johnny. Mike was a scholar, playboy and dancer. He played guard on the football team, ran track, and won the Distinguished Science Student Award. This was the time of Elvis Presley and Buddy Holly. Mike and his friends, Sam and Gary, all wore their hair slicked back in ducktails.

Tom was fearless. He was wiry and quick, with an air of rebellion and a sense of humor. Dad always said that if he got into a scrape, it was Tom he'd want behind him. Tom was like Putsy—he didn't take shit from anybody.

What I remember most clearly in relation to Mike was one of his girlfriends, Debbie Kaston. She was blond and spirited, with a straight back, an open face, and broad shoulders. She was beautiful to me. To say I had a crush on her understated the truth, like saying Babe Ruth played baseball. One summer Mike brought Debbie to the cottage for a week. He was a sophomore in college. I was ten and Debbie stayed in the bedroom next to mine. The walls upstairs at the cottage were constructed of pine boards nailed to one side of the wooden studs. Two closets were built into the common wall, one opening into each bedroom. In the inquisitive way of children, my brother Steve and I had discovered a small knot that was loose in one of the pine boards. The knot was the size of a nickel and slid neatly out of the wood, giving a perfect view through the adjoining closet into the next bedroom. Usually I couldn't see much through

The Knothole

the knothole because of clothes hanging in the closet. But now and then, if the clothes were separated just right, the line of sight was unobstructed. I hadn't looked through this knothole very often—until the week Debbie Kaston stayed at the cottage.

One day after swimming in the lake, I was in my room taking off my wet bathing suit. I heard someone come up the stairs, then the door closed in the room next to mine. After a few minutes I remembered the knothole. I wavered back and forth. Should I look through it? If I were discovered it would cause a major flap. There were probably clothes hanging in the closet, anyway, and I wouldn't be able to see a thing. The impulse to look got the best of me. I couldn't resist.

As silent and careful as a thief, I slid the pine knot out of the wall. I looked through the hole and couldn't believe my eyes. Debbie Kaston, the love of my ten-year-old life, was framed perfectly in my line of sight and she was just beginning to take off her bathing suit! My breath caught in my throat. She unzipped the back of her one-piece suit and gingerly slipped the straps over her shoulders. She'd been lying in the sun and her skin was bright pink. She pulled the suit down to her waist, fully exposing her breasts, and I nearly fainted. My eyes were riveted to her breasts like Francisco Pizarro's to the golden riches of the Incas. Debbie wriggled slightly as she pulled the bathing suit down over her hips and thighs, then she stepped out of it completely. My heart was racing. I could barely breathe. Right before my eyes, not ten feet away, stood a totally naked woman. I had never seen a naked woman before—not my mother, not my sister, no one. In my family, the private parts of bodies, especially female bodies, were kept well hidden.

I looked at Debbie, at the curve of her breasts. I had no other breasts to compare them to—I had never seen a woman's breasts before. But I loved them. They were full and pointed, with round, pinkish nipples at the tips. They jiggled slightly as she moved. In profile, they sloped down and outward like two miniature ski jumps.

Debbie turned toward me, looking at the back of her sunburned shoulder in the mirror. Her breasts faced me straight on. A patch of blond hair formed a triangle at the top of her thighs. Then she turned the other way, looking over her shoulder in the mirror, and I could see the line splitting the round curves of her buttocks. This was too much for me. I was breathing so hard I thought she would hear me. I knew I shouldn't be doing this. This spying was cowardly and dishonest. I was committing a sin of impurity—it could even be a mortal sin for all I knew—but I didn't care. All I wanted in the world was to watch this glorious, naked female body.

Debbie pressed her fingers into her shoulders and thighs, leaving white marks on her sunburned skin. She took a few steps away from me, bent over and took something from her suitcase. It was a small bottle of lotion. She poured some into her palm and began rubbing it slowly, gently, onto her shoulders and upper arms. When she finished, she spread the lotion onto her chest. She massaged it into her pink skin, then into the white skin of her breasts and stomach. Her nipples hardened and moved in mesmerizing circles as she rubbed the lotion into the soft flesh of her breasts.

The Knothole

She worked slowly down her whole body. She rubbed the lotion into her thighs, then fluffed up the hair between her legs, which was pressed into tight little curls. When she finished spreading lotion down the length of her legs, she rubbed her hands over her whole body one more time to make sure all the lotion was absorbed into her skin. From the side her rear end had a wonderful, pear-shaped curve. I couldn't take my eyes off it. I thought there could be no curve in creation so perfect as the curve of this woman's rear end. I was drawn to it as a lone pilgrim is drawn to the warmth of firelight.

Debbie bent over and took a bra and underpants from her suitcase. This was another first. I had seen bras in the laundry, but I had never seen a woman put one on before. I was fascinated by the deft and intricate ritual that followed. She slipped both arms through the straps, pulled them over her pink shoulders, arched forward while settling her full breasts into the cups, then hooked the clasps behind her back, all in one continuous motion of exquisite fluidity. It was like a short, intricate dance movement.

She turned toward me and walked to the closet. Trembling, I held my breath and watched the smooth white skin of her stomach and thighs three feet from me. She was close enough to touch.

She took clothes off a hanger and put on a pair of shorts and a loose white blouse. That fast it was all over. She was dressed. I felt like a sailor in a full wind that suddenly goes slack. I wanted to see more of her. I wanted never to take my eyes off her naked body, off her round ass and nipples and the curly hair between her legs.

I heard her door open and the click of her sandals on the stairway. I put the round knot of wood back in the hole and sat on my bed, panting. I was exhausted and teeming with energy. I hadn't known such wonder existed in the world.

I immediately thought about when I could see her again, when she might go swimming or undress. I was the youngest so I had to go to bed before everyone else. That night I lay there without a chance of sleep. When I heard footsteps on the stairs my heart started beating faster.

Debbie switched on her light and I slipped out of bed. I slid the knot out of the wall, looked through the hole, and cursed. A skirt on a hanger blocked my view. My heart sank. I could see only a small patch of the floor. Twice she passed but I could see her legs only from the knees down.

A few minutes later she stood in the same spot where she had taken off her bathing suit and rubbed the lotion on her body that afternoon. I could see just her calves, ankles and feet. One foot lifted off the floor, then the other. Her light blue bermuda shorts came into view as she stepped out of them. One foot lifted again, then the other, and she slipped off her white panties. I was beside myself. This was torture. I knew she was standing there completely naked and all I could see was her feet. I would have given my rosary blessed by Pope Pius XII to move the skirt that was blocking my view. The light clicked off and the room went black.

All I could think about was seeing her again. Over the next five days I spent hours and hours in my room, praying to catch a glimpse of her. My mother thought I was sick. When everyone was outside I snuck into Debbie's room and moved the clothes in her closet so they wouldn't obstruct my view.

I memorized every nuance and curve of her body that week. I knew the roundness and slope of her breasts, the beautiful line separating her buttocks, the fluffy triangle at the top of her legs, and the muscles coursing down her thighs and calves. I knew them all better than the palms of my own hands.

It was a week of ecstasy. A week of mystery, fascination and allure, my first glimpse at the power of a woman's body. My resolve to be a priest weakened. Priests live apart from the magic of women. I suddenly wasn't sure I liked that idea. How could I separate myself from this wonder, this treasure? The nuns taught us that human beings are created in the image and likeness of God. Now I knew that I'd seen God in the flesh.

Playing

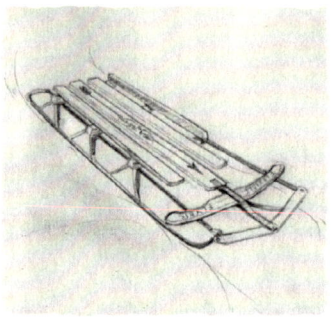

Billy Kern lived up past the Bomb Hole. The Bomb Hole was a kind of crater in the ground—maybe twenty feet across and four feet deep—atop a wooded knoll not far from our house. Billy lived over the hill, down the valley through the creekbed and up the far hill beyond. He was a friend of Steve's, a small, wiry boy with curly brown hair, dirt on his face, and the furtive look of a street mongrel. He had darting eyes and a quick, devious mind. When I thought of Billy Kern, I thought of snakes and mischief with an edge of cruelty.

The creek region a hundred yards behind his house was Billy's territory. He held dominion there. It was a wet, jungle-like, overgrown valley populated by garter snakes, frogs, raccoons, birds, insects, pollywogs and spiders. We would get as muddy as well-diggers there, build treehouses, play Tarzan and hide-and-seek, and go sledding in the winter. I spent endless hours around the creekbed, but it always spooked me. There was a murky, primordial mystery there. It was a land of "creatures," slimy things that crawled or slithered on the ground. Creatures made me nervous. I always felt like a trespasser around the creekbed, like I was being watched. It was Billy Kern's domain, and Billy Kern made me nervous.

Snakes were the source of his power. He loved snakes. They were his cousins, his brothers. The world falls into two camps: people who love snakes and people who are terrified of them. The ones who are terrified comprise perhaps ninety-nine percent of the population and I was one of them. Billy Kern knew this. In the spring and summertime I gave him a wide berth. He often carried a tangle of baby garter snakes in his pocket, all wound together in a ball. His favorite trick was to suddenly turn around and fling one onto my shoulder, or onto someone else's. He'd watch us scream and bolt in fright, then howl with laughter.

Like most boys, my brother, Steve, had a cruel streak in him. When he and Billy Kern got together they brought out the worst in each other. One time they chased my sister around the yard with snakes until she was blubbering in tears under the walnut tree. Another time they played a trick on my mother. She was in the kitchen peeling potatoes over the sink. Steve and Billy came in and hung around, talking and eating cookies, while she continued peeling potatoes. Steve got her attention, asking her to look at the scratch on his arm. While she glanced his way, Billy emptied his pocketful of snakes into the sink. When she turned back around you could hear her scream clear across the Flint River, which was three blocks away. Steve and Billy Kern were not a popular twosome around our house after that.

Timmy Phillips, who was in my class at Holy Family after we moved to Grand Blanc, reminded me of Billy Kern, except for his looks. He was a tall, skinny redhead with a face full of freckles. He also grew up next to a creek and he loved snakes and creatures. He was as comfortable with them as a Cajun in the bayou. One morning in seventh grade, in a show of manly prowess, Timmy gobbled up and swallowed two big night crawlers right before our eyes. For a week afterward I felt sick every time I looked at food.

I liked Billy Kern better in the wintertime when his slithering friends were hibernating. The hillsides behind his house that sloped down to the creekbed made the best sledding runs around. It was hard to go sledding there without getting Billy in the bargain, but in the wintertime I didn't mind so much. After school Steve and I dashed out and pulled our sleds across the snow-covered fields, up past the Bomb Hole to the hill above the creek. The sled run down that hillside was unimaginative and harrowing. It was the death run. There were no curves or traverses. It plunged straight down at a breakneck angle. At the top we would lie belly-down on our sleds, edge forward toward the precipice, teeter a moment, then hurtle downward at a thrilling, paralyzing speed. Sometimes we'd get really crazy and build a jump in the middle of the hill. We'd fly over it and end up crashing sled over heels. It's a good thing children's bones don't break easily.

My favorite sled run wound down the opposite hillside across the creek. It required more skill and finesse, which appealed to me. The track started with a gradual downslope from the base of a huge sprawling oak. We'd get a running start, belly-flop onto the sled, and shoot off down the hill. We'd steer through two easy curves, picking up speed. Then came a sharp, hard left turn—if you missed, you ended up in a gully full of thorns and had to endure everyone's ridicule. Coming out of the sharp turn, if you held it, the run plunged into a steep chute that just split two close-set oak trees, and at the bottom you had to cut a sharp right to avoid the creek. This last maneuver was more style than necessity because the creek was usually frozen over.

I had my share of triumphs and calamities. I got to know the gully like Sherlock Holmes knew Dr. Moriarity. Our relationship was adversarial. I remember one time when I negotiated the turn above the gully perfectly. I sped down the chute, split the trees, and glided around the curve at the bottom. My run was so precise and graceful that to finish with a flare I steered onto the ice, dug in the toe of my left boot and yanked on my steering bar for a 90-degree slide. It was a thing of beauty. But just as I came to a stop the ice gave way. My sled and I plunged into two feet of ice-cold water and muck. Everyone howled. By the time I got home I was nearly frozen to death.

Another time I was in trouble on the gully turn. I came in too high and fast. I was dancing on the edge, like Joey Chitwood, the stuntcar driver, teetering on two wheels. I tried desperately to dig my runners into the turn and balance back with my body so I wouldn't fly over the side. Finally I held it. I gained control and pulled the sled back into the run. But I discovered with a panic that I'd stayed up high too long to come into the chute straight. I slammed head-on into the left-hand oak tree. I crumbled, rolled off my sled and everything went black. Five minutes later I came to with four sets of eyes staring down at me. I had a headache for three days, but the fact that I'd been knocked cold was a badge of honor.

I coveted my brother's sled. This was probably only a venial sin since I wasn't coveting my neighbor's wife. Steve had a Flexible Flyer. He got it for Christmas one year. It was long and sleek with red runners and varnished wood that shined like a sailboat. It even had a shiny chrome bumper on the front—ideal for slamming into oak trees without wrecking the sled. Steve let me help him scrape the red paint off the bottom of the runners with a rock (you didn't want any paint on the runners—it would slow you down). Then he waxed them with a candle that we swiped from the manger scene of Jesus' birth that Mom always set up in the living room at Christmas.

Flexible Flyers were the Maseratis of sleds. They were exactly what their name described—flexible for sharp turning, and they could fly over the snow. They weren't stiff like most sleds. They were long, fast and maneuverable. They could make turns no other sled could make. Sometimes Steve let me take a few runs on the Flyer. What an experience, what a feeling. It was like howling along in a sleek boat with an outboard motor after paddling an old wooden canoe. If I had been on Steve's Flexible Flyer I never would have hit that oak tree—or so I told myself. Such delusions comforted me.

When it wasn't wintertime we played at the Bomb Hole. We weren't sure just how it got there, but imagined that it came from a bomb or a cannon shell during the Civil War. Perhaps some secret Rebel army circled high into Yankee territory undetected and swept down with attacks from the North. Initially they would have encountered little resistance due to the element of surprise, like the Japanese at Pearl Harbor. But when they reached Flushing the defense stiffened and cannon battles erupted. That would explain the Bomb Hole. Military history was obviously not our strong suit. But we played war games there: cowboys and Indians, the Rifleman, Davey Crockett, and World War II. We'd split up and either defend or attack the Bomb Hole, shooting imaginary bullets and arrows from our toy pistols, rifles, and bows. I later wondered if these games were good training for those of us who ended up in war for real in Vietnam.

DREAMING

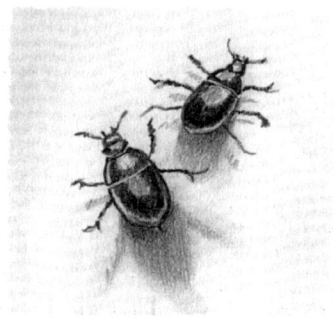

My earliest memory is of a nightmare. I was in my crib, still too young to speak. The crib was upstairs in the front bedroom where Johnny and Mike slept. It was the middle of the night. I was sleeping on my back, wearing my light blue Dr. Denton's, the flannel pajamas with the feet attached and the button-flap in back, and I had a dream.

In the dream I was located exactly where I was in reality—sleeping on my back in the crib. Except in the dream I was wide awake, looking straight upward. Next to my head, just a few inches away, were two huge black beetles. They were horrifying. They had long legs and hard, shiny black shells. They were creeping closer and closer to my head, but I couldn't move a muscle or look at them. If I did they would fly straight at my face and attack me. I was frozen with terror.

My next memory is from a few moments later. I am

Dreaming

standing in the far corner of the crib, screaming. The light flashes on and my mother rushes into the room. She holds me. I scream and point to where the bugs are. She looks to where I am pointing. Nothing is there.

"What's wrong, sweetheart? What's wrong?" she says.

I scream and point, desperate to communicate the source of my terror. The bugs are gone now, of course. They hid with all the commotion. But they'll be back.

Half the house is up now. My mother tries to comfort me but I cannot be comforted. She'll want to put me back to sleep in the crib, back where the bugs are. I try to tell her, to make her understand, but I cannot yet speak! I have the thoughts but no words. It's like wanting to run but having no legs to run on. I feel a wrenching frustration at my inability to communicate. I desperately want to tell her about the bugs, the huge black hardshell bugs, but I cannot say words. I cannot make them understand. All I can do is scream and point in my terror and frustration.

Each time my mother tries to put me back in the crib I scream louder. Finally, she takes me to her room and nestles me between her and my father. At last I calm down. I am safe here. The bugs cannot get me.

How are our terrors born, the fears that haunt us? What is the trigger? Does a void without fear exist within us initially, which later is filled by the memory of pain so that fear then aids our survival, as with a child burning its finger? Why does fear burgeon into irrationality? Does acrophobia come from falling out of a tree as a child? Or from falling dreams? Or are we born with it? Was I born with my fear of large, hard-shelled insects? The dream terrorized me, but to have been so frightened the fear must have lived in me beforehand. Did I experience some trauma even earlier that seeded this dread in me? The fear (shall I call it phobia?) has remained even into adulthood.

Mike and Stacy Smithson, my playmates as a child, lived five houses away around the corner, but through backyards and over fences was the only way we traveled to each others' houses. We played ball in their backyard, hide-and-seek into the dark hours of the night, and in winter we skated, went sledding, and threw snowballs till our hands froze.

One summer when I was eight or nine, Mr. Smithson parked a long wooden trailer with high sides behind his garage. We played games inside. It became a sailing ship, a fort, a space ship and a railroad car. One day we found an army-green tarpaulin in the garage, threw it over the trailer and played army. Then we decided to "sleep out" that night in the trailer, covered-wagon style. We wrangled permission from our parents, gathered sleeping bags and set up for our adventure, six of us together, crossing the broad western plains through Indian country.

When darkness fell, after the hamburger roast and hide-and-seek, we secured our imaginary 20-mule team and retired inside the covered wagon, guns close within reach. We took turns standing watch for a surprise attack by the wily Cheyenne—twice we'd seen a lone scout on a distant ridge line earlier in the day. As the lantern light steadied, we took out the cards and matchsticks to play poker. And

Dreaming

as sometimes happens on warm early summer nights in Michigan, after darkness settled in, the June bugs came.

We heard a small thud against the tarpaulin cover, then another, and another, like intermittent hail stones. Then a dark brown, shiny, hardshelled June bug, two inches long, landed squarely in front of me as I was about to discard. I knocked over the table as I leapt back in terror. The others laughed at my fright.

I hated June bugs. They were first cousins to the tormentors in my crib dream. I can still remember the pinging sound as they struck the screens of my bedroom window on a summer night. After I jumped away from the table inside our covered wagon, I heard more thuds against the tarp and pictured the scene outside. We had secured the cover well in case it rained, but there were small cracks at the corners. A few minutes later another June bug landed inside, and I was turning inside out. I knew I couldn't stay here all night. I would go mad.

I told the others I was leaving. They said what kind of a cowboy was I? If we were out on the range there'd be a lot more than June bugs to deal with. I said I didn't care. We weren't out on the range and I could deal with lots of things, but June bugs weren't one of them.

But I had to get home. And to get home I had to go outside, into the torrent of June bugs. It was like being on a sinking boat surrounded by sharks and knowing that the only way to get to land was by swimming through the water.

I wrapped my sleeping bag tight around me, especially around my head and neck. The more I heard the Junebugs thud against the tarp the more terrified I became.

But I had to go. I couldn't stay here. I tried to steel my courage. I threw open the trailer's back gate and plunged into the darkness.

June bugs were everywhere. I felt them pelt against the sleeping bag. I raced half-screaming around the garage and crossed the driveway. June bugs crunched under my feet. The ground was covered with them. The crunching sound made my skin crawl. I tripped jumping over a fence and sprawled headlong into the grass. I felt bugs crawling over my hands. One got inside my shirt and I screamed.

Finally I made it home. It felt like the longest run of my life. I remembered watching a horror movie in which a man is trapped inside a cave of bats, which are the creatures that terrify him the most. He goes crazy and his hair turns white. When I got upstairs, panting, I looked in the mirror to see if my hair had changed color. When I went to sleep that night I prayed that I wouldn't have any dreams.

Ancestors

I was about seven when Grandpa died. This was another aspect of my advancement to the Age of Reason, I supposed. Not only could I now commit mortal sins and burn in hell, but the people I loved could die. I never heard anyone refer to Grandpa as "Grandpa Damm," to distinguish him from another grandparent, because by the time I was born all my other grandparents had already left the living. So whenever "Grandpa" was mentioned, we all knew immediately who was being talked about.

I realize now, looking at old pictures, that Dad and Grandpa looked a lot alike. This surprises me because I had never noticed it before. They were both big men, over six feet tall and thick in the neck, head, and torso. Grandpa had a full head of snow white hair, as did Dad in his later years. And there was a similarity in the shape and light in their eyes, the line of the nose, a certain wry smile that sometimes crossed their faces.

Now and then in the summertime Grandpa would drive up from his home in Ohio to visit us at the cottage. Dad would take a week off from work, which was unusual, but other than that, when Grandpa came to visit our days at the lake were the same as usual.

We kids water-skied or fished, mowed the grass, played touch football or shagged ground balls in the side yard, or played cards, Clue, or Monopoly inside if it rained. Mom cooked a lot and did laundry—which she always did—and for dinner Dad would grill chicken, hamburgers, or fresh fish (depending on our luck on the lake). Grandpa always took a swim if the weather was nice, and he liked to sit on the front porch or outside on a white wooden lawn chair and look out at the water. He and Dad were alike in that as well.

I loved it when Grandpa took me on a drive with him. He liked being around all the activity with the family and kids, but then he'd reach a point where he needed some peace and quiet. He had lived alone for many years and all the commotion was just too much for him. Sometimes he'd go off by himself for an hour or two, but every so often he would say to me: "Would you like to go for a drive with me, Petie?"

"Could I, Grandpa? That would be great," I'd say excitedly.

Grandpa loved to drive. He would sit behind the wheel of his big Oldsmobile (all the cars were big in those days) and look like a duke out for a spin in the country. After awhile he'd glance over and say: "Would you like to drive?"

It was the question I was waiting, waiting, hoping to hear. "Wow, could I, Grandpa? Could I drive?" This was like asking me if I wanted a pirate's chest full of gold doubloons, or a ride on Silver, the Lone Ranger's horse.

"Well, sure you can. But only if you're a good driver. Will you be a good driver?"

"Oh, yes, sir, I sure will. I'll be a real good driver."

Grandpa pulled over to the side of the road and hoisted me onto his lap in front of the steering wheel. I'd grip the wheel at ten and two o'clock just like he'd taught me. He'd have me look in the rearview mirror to see if any cars were coming (there never were), then we would pull back onto the road. Grandpa would accelerate to about 35 mph (he worked the gas and brake pedals since my feet came nowhere near them) and we would glide down the gentle curves and straightaways of Platte Road. We'd go by the big field with jet black soil where onions grew, and by the stand of tall trees where an old eagle's nest perched in the weathered gray branches of a dead spruce. What a feeling it was driving that car, sitting on Grandpa's lap and steering like we were going all the way to Montana. We'd go down to the end of Platte Road where it joined highway M-22. Sometimes Grandpa would turn the car around and head back the other way, still letting me steer, before he would drive us into Honor or Beulah and buy me an ice cream cone. He made me promise that this was our little secret together and I couldn't tell a soul. My mom and dad would get real mad if they knew I was driving a car just like an adult. Only much later did I realize that all the while I was "driving," Grandpa had his hand on the bottom of the wheel.

I remember looking at Grandpa as he lay in his casket. He looked calm and restful, like he was just taking a nap, except he was all dressed up in a white shirt, tie, and a blue suit coat. His white hair was perfectly combed. Mom and I went up to the casket together in the parlor at the funeral home. Mom knelt down on the kneeler padded with red velvet, but I stood up on it, because otherwise I too short to see Grandpa. While she said some prayers I looked at him, resting there so peacefully. I reached out and touched his cheek, and reflexively, pulled my hand away. His cheek was cold, and felt like it was made of wax. After a few seconds I reached out and touched it again, and in that moment I knew what dead was. I had never seen, let alone touched, a dead person before, and now...Grandpa.

"Will Grandpa come to see us at the cottage next summer, Mommy" I asked.

"No, he won't be coming to the cottage anymore. Grandpa's gone to be with the angels now."

Ancestors

"Is Grandpa dead?"
"Yes, sweetie. Grandpa's dead."
I knew she was going to say that, and I started crying.

When Dad was in his early seventies I realized that I knew very little about my parents' early lives and our family history. One of my favorite things on earth is to spend autumn in the northwoods when the leaves are turning, so every October I would journey back to Platte Lake to visit Mom and Dad and watch the leaves change. One year—after much cajoling and prodding—they agreed to sit down with a tape recorder and talk about their histories, about our ancestry.

We talked in the living room in front of the fireplace, and as Dad spoke, his right hand tapped an intermittent rhythm on the arm of his leather chair, as it often did when he told some kind of story. Grandpa was born in 1883 in Cleveland where his father owned a saloon. The saloon was called "Damm's" and was the main meeting place for the neighborhood. Grandpa was one of three sons (his brother, Adam, later became city treasurer in Cleveland). Dad's grandparents on his mother's side grew up in poor farming families in Bavaria and immigrated to this country about the time of the Civil War. They met over here, near Cleveland, but had come, it turned out, from villages (the names of which Dad didn't know) located just a few miles apart back in Bavaria. They married, worked hard, had 16 children (German Catholics), and were able eventually to buy a farm that grew in size over the years.

Dad was the second of six kids, and he remembered

his whole family going out to his grandparents' farm for Sunday afternoon dinners. These were large gatherings with lots of cousins, aunts and uncles. Chickens or a hog were butchered in the morning to go with homemade breads, pies, and other dishes. In the cellar were big crocks of sauerkraut and barrels of wine made from grapes grown on the farm.

I asked Dad if he knew why these ancestors had come to the United States in the first place.

"To escape the Prussian Army," he said.

"Escape the Prussian Army? What was going on?"

The Prussians ruled a large area of what is now Germany and Poland. They were engaged in various wars and campaigns and desperately needed soldiers. So they swept through the countryside and forcibly conscripted young men into the Prussian Army. Word spread across the land before them and a lot of young men and families fled to America—usually with almost nothing because they had to leave quickly—rather than staying to die in the Prussian wars.

"That's how your great grandparents got here."

The University of Michigan was politically aflame in the late 1960s when I was a student there. The Vietnam War was tearing the country apart and Ann Arbor was at the center of the rift. There were teach-ins, demonstrations and marches, smashed windows at banks and businesses and confrontations with police. Students at Kent State were gunned down by the National Guard and demonstrators beaten at the Democratic Convention in Chicago in 1968. Cassius Clay, now converted to Islam and named Muhammad

Ali, was stripped of his heavyweight boxing crown and arrested for refusing, on religious grounds, induction into the U.S. Army.

My life at Michigan existed both on the periphery and near the vortex of this tumult. I was not by nature political, despite my father's long political engagement, but to be in Ann Arbor at this time was to be surrounded by unease and protest. Vietnam permeated the air like smoke rising from a fire.

Registration for the draft was compulsory for all young men. You got a letter from the draft board and you went down to register. It was the law. I drove to a dingy building in Flint and filled out the forms. It forced me to think about war in a way I never had before, because now at age eighteen I was on the list of potential soldiers. I might have to carry a gun, to kill other people, or be killed or maimed myself. Even then, though, I felt a margin of safety. I knew I was off to the University of Michigan in the fall and would have a student deferment. If a young man had ambivalence about going to college in 1967 or '68, the student deferment from the draft wiped away the indecision, because it was pretty much school or boot camp and Vietnam. We all knew the rules for maintaining our draft deferment, how many units we had to carry each semester and such. Certain things in school you could mess up with little consequence — the draft deferment was not among them.

I wondered sometimes what I would do if I lost my deferment and were drafted. At Michigan we often talked about the war. Some guys said they would seek conscientious objector status if they were drafted. Others would create real or fake injuries, or fake mental derangement, to get declared 4-F—medically unfit to serve. Still others were very clear that they would leave the country, go to Canada or Sweden. Some even had escape plans already in place if that were ever necessary. I was not so clear. We didn't really talk about the war in my family, much less about options for avoiding the draft. But without ever discussing it, I knew as surely as Platte Lake froze in the wintertime that if I were drafted, Dad would want me to go. This wasn't Bavaria with the Prussian Army sweeping through. This was America, and you obeyed and fought for freedom.

  I remember participating in an anti-war rally on The Diag, the main square on campus, one afternoon. People were crowded shoulder to shoulder. Speakers spoke passionately into the microphone against the war, against the draft, against the killing. Young men waved their draft cards in the air, back and forth, and shouted, "No more war! No more war!" Then cigarette lighters came out all over The Diag and people yelled, "Burn them! Burn them!" Soon flames were rising from burning draft cards like small torches lifted to the sky. I held my draft card in my hand, the student next to me held out his lighter, and at the last moment I couldn't do it. I knew then that if I got drafted I would go. I would fight the war, not because I supported it, or supported the government. But because if I didn't I would shame my father. I would go off to war instead.

  How ironic, I thought nearly twenty years later, listening to Dad tell the story of how my forebears came to America to avoid conscription into the Prussian Army. We are the descendants of draft dodgers.

Leaving

Dad and I did not always agree. Did not see eye to eye, so to speak. I had difficulty knowing what I wanted "to do in life." My brothers John, Mike, and Steve all knew from a young age that they wanted to be doctors. They went to Catholic colleges, enrolled in pre-med courses straightaway, and advanced on to medical school, John and Mike after only three years of study. I, on the other hand, had no clue, and I both envied and loathed my brothers' certitude.

I grew up assuming that I would pursue either law or medicine. Those seemed to me the extent of my choices. Dad had been a practicing attorney his entire adult life, my other brother, Tom, went to law school, John, Mike, and Steve were on their way or already doctors, and Susan was a nurse. So when people asked me: "What are you going to be?" I said: "Oh, a doctor or a lawyer, I guess." This was the modern analogue of hereditary apprenticeship, of the son following the father or older brother into the blacksmith shop, cobblering, glass blowing or the farmer's field.

But law and medicine presented problems. I didn't like science, detested math, and blood and human anatomy were exceptionally low on my favorite-things list. The intricacies, minutiae, stratagems, and confrontation of the law left me as inspired as a dead lily pad on the bottom of a pond. So at the end of my first year at the University of Michigan I confronted an empty chasm. The administrators said I had to "declare a major." This felt to me like leaping into a wide and dangerous unknown, because to commit to something in that way had meaning, it carried weight, and one had to follow the path. So I refused. This didn't make them happy. "Look," they said, "you have to put SOMETHING down." But I didn't. I kept searching, taking classes. By the end of my second year, they were extremely not pleased. "You MUST declare a major in order to continue at this university," they insisted. So, pushed to this particular edge, and still having no clear idea, I did a dumb thing. I declared TWO majors: English Literature and Speech. What I enjoyed most was writing. But not research papers, not scholarly texts. I could care less about the meter of Shakespeare's sonnets or the symbolism of dark plumage in the stories of Edgar Allen Poe. I liked to write what I thought of as "my own work." Fiction, short stories, poems. A great way to make a living one day. Right.

I eventually garnered enough sense to whittle my double major down to a single one in literature with a minor in speech, so I was able to graduate (with Honors) on time in four years. I returned home to work for the summer—five months, it turned out—on a road construction crew, which is what I had done the previous summers to make money for school. It was hot work, sixty, seventy, sometimes eighty hours a week in the humidity and hot sun. But the money was good.

My "future plans" were where the disagreements with Dad began. "Now that you have graduated, what are your future plans?" he asked me one evening.

I had anticipated this question for some days, practiced my response, and envisioned—with more than a little trepidation—his reaction. "Well," I said, stammering a bit, trying to keep my voice steady. "I'm going to work the road construction job till the fall, save as much money as possible, then go traveling in Europe."

This declaration was met with some seconds of silence and a jaw slightly agape. Then with: "You're going to WHAT?"

His reaction did not surprise me. I was twenty-two years old. When he was my age the year was 1932 and the country—the world—were deep in Depression. How could I waste my time like this, he said. I had already played around for four years in school (OUCH—though it was true, if I were honest). I should be getting serious about life, about a career. I should be saving my money. I would be starting a family sometime soon. How was I going to support them? Travel in Europe? Was I nuts?

"Start a family?" I said. I didn't even have a girlfriend. Nor did I want one at this point in my life. And the last thing I wanted was to be married. This was 1971, not 1932.

I wanted to see the world. This was part of MY education. And I was going, no matter what he said! And he could like it or not. That was his choice.

Variations of this argument raged on for most of the summer. I had never stood up to him like this before and he didn't like it. But I was determined. Finally, sometime in August, a steely silence set in as Dad realized he could not change my mind.

The glass was thick in the windows next to the doors exiting the airport in Frankfurt, Germany. It was early October. A foreboding chill was in the air and rain pelted down outside. I was traveling alone. I had never been out of the U.S. in my life. I had barely been out of Michigan. This was the third time I had ever been on an airplane, the first two being a trip to Dallas, Texas and back to visit a friend when I was a junior at Michigan (paid for by the winnings from an all-night poker game when I should have been studying for a Business Law exam). It was six o'clock in the morning. A gray-black day was dawning and I was exhausted from the long flight across the Atlantic.

Frankfurt, Germany. I didn't know a soul here. I didn't speak a word of German. I had come because it was the cheapest flight to Europe I could find. For the longest time I stood there, watching the rain pour down in the gray light, feeling utterly alone on an unknown continent, and thinking: "What the hell have I done?"

There are worse things in life than wandering the shores of Greek islands. If it was good enough for Byron it was okay for me. Christmas and New Year's found me in Agios Nikolaos, a small fishing village on the east end of Crete. After Frankfurt I hooked up with an old roommate from Ann Arbor, Pete Newell, or Nasty Newell, as I called him. Nasty was 6'4", 250 pounds, a former All Big Ten defensive tackle, a philosophy major and one of the sweetest people alive. We visited Amsterdam and Paris, bought an old gray Peugeot 505 and toured the French countryside, Geneva and the Swiss Alps, Vienna, and skied in Innsbruck (my first time on snow skis). We left the car in Trieste, Italy and moved south by train through Tito's Yugoslavia to the age-old beauty of Greece.

We had no itinerary. We moved about on the soft currents of impulse, weather, and travelers' stories about wonderful places to visit, like fishermen passing rumors back and forth about where the fish are biting. After my initial dislocation and malaise, I had grown to love this traveling. The new languages, the cultures, ruins, French pastries, ancient cathedrals, Rhine wine, mountain hamlets, the ALPS! for Christsakes. We don't have mountains in Michigan. The Louvre. The Rodin Museum. People from around the world. New friends from Rhodesia, France, Australia, Italy. I could feel myself growing, blossoming, worlds away from Grand Blanc.

In Agios Nikolaos a rock promontory jutted into the Aegean and formed part of the outer rim of the cove where the village nestled against the sea. We knew it was cold and probably snowing back in the Midwest, but during the sun-washed afternoons we would walk to The Rock, as we called it, and swim in the clear sea. The water was a rich turquoise hue that I had never seen, but imagined one might find on exotic islands in the Caribbean or South Pacific. I would stand on a ledge fifteen feet above the water, look down and see black sea urchins twenty feet below the surface as clearly as if they sat on a table just in front of me. Then I'd push off, do swan dives and half twists into the pristine water, and think of Billy Johnson at the YMCA.

We watched the fishermen bring in their catches, drank ouzo, retsina, and ate seafood so flavorful it made you weep. We read books, listened to the Greeks play their music, watched them dance their dances, and wandered the island's rocky cliffs and historical sites. Knossos, one of the centers of Minoan civilization, was nearby. It was a startling experience to walk among those ruins, feeling the presence and imagining the lives of Bronze Age people from 5000 YEARS AGO, who walked on, lived on, worked on these very rocks beneath my feet.

Nasty decided it was time to leave and make his way home to Chicago. His money was running low. He'd had enough of the road and was ready to start looking for a job. I stayed. I wasn't sure where this journey would lead next, but I knew my traveling wasn't over.

Part II
Moonrise

WEATHER

In my mid-twenties, after stints in Britain, India, Colorado and Michigan, I moved to Northern California. There is a "wet season" and a "dry season" in California. In wintertime the rains stream down outside. The hills are as green as Ireland. Pink plum blossoms line the streets in early February and the green shoots of daffodils and tulips poke up through the dirt. The air is moist and light. It's a pleasant alternative to ten degrees below zero and months of snow.

But the "dry season" in California unsettles me. It fills me with foreboding and unease. Day after day is beautiful and sunny, but during the six or seven months from mid-April through October rain will fall once, maybe twice. The aesthetics still jar me, even decades later. By June the hills have all turned "golden." I think of them as brown. They look to me as if they've died. But when the rains return in winter the hills turn green and lush again. I can never believe that they come back to life. Without water plants die. But these don't. They are like bears in winter.

When I was twelve and we moved from Flushing to the farm outside of Grand Blanc, I became more attuned to nature's cycles and power. In wintertime I understood how the town got its name from French trappers: Grand Blanc, the Big White. Snow stretched unbroken to the horizon. After the thaw and spring rains, when the fields finally dried enough, the farmers plowed the broad expanses with tractors, folding last year's brown weals and crop remains back into the earth. Then the heavy clods of dark soil were cut finer by sharp-bladed disc harrows, the soil furrowed neatly into rows, and the seeds planted that began the miracle of another year's crop. They planted wide fields of corn, wheat, alfalfa and soybeans. For the next five months I watched the fields change. Planting is an act of faith. Farmers put their small seeds of salvation into the ground and hope. At first a stillness and quiet covered the landscape, an eerie changelessness that grew almost tense. Gradually minute green blades appeared, like scouts, a few here, a few there. Then suddenly, as if on signal, the fields were awash with green.

The plants broadened and grew. Leaves unfurled. Before long the corn stalks grew as high as my knee, then my waist. But always there existed that key element, the lifeblood of growth—rain. Water. Fate resided in the sky. The farmers looked skyward as if by reflex. Endless sunny days were a curse. I watched the grass of the lawn around our house, which I had to mow. It was my gauge. If the grass was green, all was well. If the grass turned brown, then browner, the farmers became desperate. Brown grass in the middle of summer was a sign of death. It meant that the crops would shrivel and die. It meant that people went broke or couldn't feed their families in winter. No rain meant drought. There were no fancy irrigation systems where I came from.

So I find the "dry season" in California unsettling. It makes me wince. I still can't look at the "golden" hills without feeling uneasy. The golden still looks brown to me.

Weather always affected me more powerfully than I realized. As with many things, I recognized this only by contrast. The seasons were as unconscious and integral a part of me as is a fish's taking oxygen from the water it swims in. Often a disturbance occurs when a person raised in one climate moves to a different one. We can't anticipate the effects because we can't conceive of the changes. We have never experienced the differences and usually don't understand the strength of the fabric that weaves us together.

I arrived in California in February, the "rainy season," as I discovered later. I traveled up the Coast Highway from Southern to Northern California. The scenery was breathtaking. I stayed overnight in a town called Cayucos because the hills reminded me of western Scotland and the Isle of Skye. They were green, treeless and primal, yet soft as broad carpets. I slept in an old motel, and in the middle of the night, freezing, I turned on the ancient electric-coil wall heater. An hour later I was wheezing and unable to breathe, gripped in the only asthmatic attack of my life. Every time I breathed in, instead of my lungs filling, a frightening, constricted wheeze issued from my throat and chest, as if some devil were alive inside me. I couldn't get enough air. I thought I would die in that bed. I grabbed my sleeping bag and coat. I nearly stumbled out the door. It was pouring down rain outside, so dark I could barely see. I found a pier near the ocean and crawled underneath it, heaving for breath. Water soaked through the bag, but after a while my breathing eased. The sensation of my guts pulling inside out finally stopped. Since that night I have understood the asthmatic's torture.

Shortly after I arrived in Northern California I visited a half-dozen old friends I knew from Ann Arbor. They lived together on a 200-acre ranch near Bodega Bay, an hour and a half north of San Francisco. The ranch had been in one of their families for five generations, since the days of Kit Carson. I felt an immediate kinship with this place. Two hundred acres was the same size as the farm I'd grown up on. From one of the ridgelines I could see the ocean, and the hills were a lush green, the color of life to me.

At dinner I learned that two of the people living there, Tom and Jane, were getting married that summer, on June 22nd. The ceremony would be held beneath a huge live oak tree near the back of the ranch. Afterward, the reception would be outside, up near the main house.

"Congratulations," I toasted. Everyone drank. "How many people will be here?" I asked.

"Oh, probably 150," Tom said.

I looked around. The house was not very large.

"That's a lot of people," I said. "What are your contingency plans?"

Weather

Jane looked at Tom.

"What do you mean, 'contingency plans?'" she said.

"Well, for the weather. In case it rains. If you're planning an outdoor wedding with 150 people you'd better have a place for them to go in case it rains."

Everyone looked at each other and softly smiled.

"Don't worry, it won't rain," Tom said.

"It won't rain? June 22nd is four months away. How can you know it's not going to rain four months from now?"

Tom chuckled.

"Trust me," he said. "It isn't going to rain."

I couldn't understand their blind faith, their lack of concern.

"How can you be so sure?"

"Because it doesn't rain here in June."

Now I chuckled.

"What do you mean, it doesn't rain here in June?"

"There is a wet season and a dry season in California. It stops raining in about mid-April and doesn't rain again until October or November."

He said this without a trace of mystery or drama, as if it were simply true, a fact. I couldn't comprehend such an idea.

"It doesn't rain for six months?" I said, utterly incredulous.

"Nope."

"Doesn't everything die?"

"No. The plants have adapted over the centuries. In the summertime the hills and fields turn a beautiful golden color."

I thought about no rain for six months and got edgy.

There was something unnatural and depraved about it, a corruption of the natural order. How could all these grasses I saw around me, lush and verdant with life, receive no rain for six months and not die? And what must such utter predictability do to the psyches of the people here?

In Michigan we have an old adage: If you don't like the weather, wait ten minutes and it will change. Like most maxims, it is founded on truth. Wind, rain, sunshine, thunderstorms, cloudiness, hot spells, cold spells alternate with the unpredictability of tornadoes in springtime. You never know from dawn to dusk what the next two hours might bring. This creates an unconscious flexibility in the people. One must retain a capacity to adjust. The unexpected, the unknown (both positive and negative), are an accepted part of everyday life. Early on, one realizes that many things lie beyond our control. From this a certain humility accrues.

Summers during college I worked as a grade checker on road construction crews. We didn't do the paving, but the "dirt work," the earth moving with big bulldozers and heavy equipment. We were very vulnerable to mud. It stopped us dead. So we were always conscious of crowning the fills and cutting ditches for drainage. Every day before quitting time all the work areas were graded or sloped so any water from rainstorms would drain off. In all the years I worked there, only once did we not do the end-of-the-day grading. We had a deadline to meet. Everyone was exhausted from working 12- to 14-hour days, seven days a week. The weatherman was emphatic. There was zero chance of rain for the next two days. It was already 8:00 pm, there wasn't a cloud in the sky, and we'd be back at 5:30 in the morning. Rather than spend another hour cutting drainage, we decided to go home. At midnight the skies opened up and we were shut down for a week, unable to move in the mud.

Tom was right. June 22nd arrived, the day of the wedding. Sure enough, the skies were bright blue without a hint of rain.

They say our bodies naturally crave the essential nutrients in which we become deficient. It is a survival mechanism by which we stay in balance. A similar mechanism operates in me regarding weather. I have essential needs. An emotional component in my psyche recognized, before my mind did, that where I live in California thunderstorms never belt out their magic roar and fire. Every three or four years I hear a tiny gurgle of thunder. These are like the whimpers of a week-old cub compared to the roar of old-lion thunder I heard as a child. Such thunder strangely soothes me. I love it. Thunderstorms let me know that the natural world is out there, powerful and unfettered as it should be. When this force is gone I feel that something is amiss and out of balance.

California has no real autumn. It also has no winter, except in the mountains. But the loss of autumn is a terrible price to pay for the giant gain of avoiding miserable winters. The two are inextricably linked. Without the icy cold of winter the trees don't need to slip into the slumber that gives us fall.

Autumn is in my blood. It is instinctual, part of my rhythm, bred into me with the same power that sends the caribou southward with the frost. When late September and October arrive I feel a potent agitation. I experience an almost physiological need to be amidst trees that are changing colors, to walk in the autumn forest. This is a feeling beyond my ability to describe. It is memory, connection, reverence and sensation. There exists in those trees for that short span of time a mixture of color and light, dryness and moisture, chill, warmth and foreboding that moves me to silent awe. It portends death while being unshakably bound to a basic force of life and renewal.

September and October are the hottest months of the year in Northern California. It is a time when all my instincts tell me the days should be growing cooler. Breezes should rise. Instead the air gets still. Inversion layers descend, the temperatures climb to the nineties, and smog settles like smoke in a closed room. This only increases my autumn agitation. I feel like a husky in the tropics. Animals acclimatize over millennia. Contrary to much current belief, we humans are animals too. My ancestors are Northern European: Irish, English and German. I don't cope well with heat. Autumn forests and chill have been bred into me for a thousand years. So when October comes I begin my annual migration. I go off to Michigan, New England, upstate New York — anywhere it's autumn. I walk in the forests, paddle the streams and listen to the thunder roar. My instincts are satisfied, my deficiencies healed. My world comes back toward balance.

Father

May 10

A month ago, while my father was doing nothing he can specifically identify, the large bone in his thigh spontaneously broke. A cancerous lesion had eaten away its strength.

    He didn't know the bone was broken. There was no "event," no fall. Over subsequent days the pain gathered, like a hurricane building at sea before it ravages the land. Even standing became difficult. He would go up the staircase to his bedroom backward, sitting on each step and lifting himself upward with his arms to keep weight off the leg. Finally, the pain won out. As he was going up the stairs the pain paralyzed him and he screamed beneath its power. He could not move in either direction, could not move his leg at all, even with my mother's help. The ambulance came. His thigh bone had split apart. Cancer is eating him bone by bone, like termites eating the beams of a house.

The doctors performed major surgery. They inserted a foot-long steel rod into the marrow of the bone to hold his leg together. Now, four weeks later, the leg is healing. Dad is home again. When he was in the hospital they wheeled him to physical therapy each day where he learned to use a walker and protect the break. His body needs time to embrace the steel. The lesion is irradiated. This is a delicate balance, trying to nurture the body and kill the cancer.

Dad's spirits are good—excellent, even. He sensed the leg's growing weakness and is glad the break is over, that it happened in southern Michigan, near the hospital and his eldest doctor-son, instead of two months later in the northwoods. The cancer has appeared elsewhere—in his spine, shoulder and lung. But this lesion in his thigh was the worst. Perhaps the spread will slow. The doctors are going to try a new chemotherapy. Everyone is hopeful.

He improves. The leg grows stronger, less painful. With the walker he can slowly get around. Stairs are the most difficult but he can negotiate a few slowly and carefully. He even drives to the hospital by himself for the radiation treatments. Spring has arrived. Flowers are blooming everywhere and each day the leg feels stronger. Soon he and my mother will go up north to the lake.

"I could get around without the walker if I had to," he tells me proudly on the phone, "but the doctor wants me to use it for another few months, just to be safe."

He wants to be his old self, carrying wood, mowing the lawn, shopping for the family food. He does not tolerate dependency well.

At last the radiation treatments end. The shooting

pains have stopped. He is pronounced strong enough to head northward to Platte Lake. His spirit resides there in the boards, the trees, the blades of grass. He has labored over and loved them for 35 years. The day they drive up with my sister, I feel his exhilaration all the way from California, as he breathes the air and looks out over Platte Lake and the forests that encircle it.

The next evening I get a call from Susan.

"Dad broke his arm," she says, "just below the shoulder." My heart sinks. Pictures flash through my mind. He must have fallen on the concrete stairs going up to the back door.

"How did it happen?"

"He was opening a jar of sauerkraut— trying to unscrew the cap—and the bone just snapped."

I am stunned. The bone just snapped, opening a jar? His body is disintegrating, being eaten away. Now he's immobilized. His leg is too fragile for him to walk without a walker, and he can't use the walker with only one arm. Now he can't even get out of bed or go to the bathroom by himself.

"How is he taking it?" I ask my sister.

She is quiet for a moment.

"He just laid his head down on the table. He's very depressed."

June 17

I sit at 30,000 feet over the deserts of Nevada en route back to Michigan, where the anchor of my life is dying. Dad's limbs are broken. He is confined to bed and a wheelchair, this physical, virile man who lettered in four sports and possessed the strength of a tree.

I look down at my own arms. I am thinner than I was as a youth, and I was never big: 142 pounds as an all-conference defensive back in high school. I had speed, quickness, brains and a quiet but pulsating determination of which even I was not fully aware. Now I am 135. My body fat is that of a miler. But I am weaker, more fragile than I was 30 years ago. My shoulders bend forward more each year, the hairs whiten in my beard. But my bones are not as brittle as a pretzel stick. My arm has not snapped opening a jar of sauerkraut.

In the distance, near the mountains that rise in Western Colorado, I see the first high, puffy clouds that always remind me of Michigan. One rises like a mushroom cloud, jarring me from a reverie in which the thought of bombs did not intrude. The valleys below are green, unlike the reds and tans of Nevada. Snow still whitens the crests of low peaks, and farther in the distance, the monolithic white of the Rocky Mountains stands stark against the blue sky. I think of wagon trains crossing this mammoth expanse a mere 100+ years ago, taking months for the journey, and of my own pilgrimage eastward—4 hours and 13 minutes at five hundred seventy nine miles per hour. My mind catches for a moment at the contrast. Can the human psyche, forged slowly over 200,000 years, survive this sudden crash of speed and technology? I look about me and wonder. The wagon train traveled 12 miles a day. My father is 76 years old. Horsedrawn carriages were a major mode of transport when he was born. I approach Michigan at 579 mph, and my father slides slowly toward the dust from which he came.

June 18

It is 9:15 pm, nearly sunset on Platte Lake. Many years have passed since I have been here in June. I'd forgotten how long the days are. The Summer Solstice is three days away. It is almost 9:30 and the sun has not yet set. The sky is bright blue and deepens toward cobalt as the sun descends. Already the moon, three-quarters full, is a white ball rising in the eastern sky. Last night I watched the sunset until 10:30 and walked in the soft moon-sun light.

I am out on the lake, drifting slowly over the weed bed where the Platte River enters the lake, near where Lee hooked the muskie. The water is as silent and reflective as glass. Not a whisper of wind stirs the surface. All around me, every five or ten seconds, fish break the water, feeding on insects. Concentric ripples emanate from their half-jumps, which sound like a single, small wave lapping the shoreline. I am silent and startled as a fish jumps five feet from my small boat. They jump more frequently now, every second or two, sometimes 3 or 4 at once. Sound surrounds me.

I glance up and see a black object streak into the water like a meteor. There is a large splash. A moment later a kingfisher rises from the water, shaking out its crowned head. Its beak and talons are empty. It ascends to a height of about forty feet and halts in mid-air, wings flapping, stationary like a humming-bird. It hovers there for fully ten seconds, gazing downward. Seeing nothing, it flies laterally another twenty yards, where it pulls up again, stationary in mid-air, wings flapping, its body curved and vertical to the water like a crescent moon. Suddenly its posture changes, the crown feathers pull in tight and the bird hurtles itself at the surface. Another splash. The kingfisher rises again from the water, struggling more this time, pulled down by the weight of a fish in its claws.

The sun is a huge, crimson oval sinking slowly beyond the trees. The full expanse of the lake extends before me, reflecting the brilliant yellow orange sky. Slowly it changes to deep gold. A pink hue rises from the tree line, followed by red, then scarlet. The colors are arresting in their pure beauty. The cloud striations turn to a deep, purple-gray. I have seen a thousand sunsets, but am struck by the scene around me. I look back toward the east and the moon lights the sky with a cool silvery glow. Seagulls circle in the dusk overhead. The fish still jump, but intermittently now. I hear a sudden clamor to my right, a clapping, honking sound from the shoreline by the river's mouth. I peer into the gathering darkness and see the white spray from wing tips slapping the water. Abruptly the clapping ceases as the white spray dies away, leaving only the honking sound to fill the air as four longneck Canadian geese, nearly black in the twilight, sweep by me thirty feet away.

June 20

The accoutrements of dying—an aluminum walker, wheel-chair, a handrail support system that fits over the toilet, a plastic in-the-bed urinal.

Father

Dad lies on his back about 22 hours a day. Even with a specially constructed mattress, bed sores plague his lower spine and buttocks. He reads, dozes, watches television, reads, gives orders, and vents frustration at the loss of control over his life. His mind is as quick as ever, his body as fragile as a robin's egg.

This breaking down is like a foe, an uneasy chamber mate. It is relentless and without compassion. It simply marches forward a step at a time, like the clock, like our lives. Sometimes Dad duels with it. Other times he turns and walks on with it, arm in arm, unresisting but smiling, enjoying the festivity that is his life even as the candle burns lower. Other times the breaking down knocks him over and drags him by the collar, choking, toward the destination around the bend.

I don't think of death as a sinister demon with the Grim Reaper's sickle. It seems more like a place to me. A place one goes that is safer than this life. Less troubled and painful. But I am not dying as acutely as my father. He may have other feelings, as I might when my time comes. He doesn't speak to me of this, but I see the fear in his eyes.

I look at a wedding photo of my parents. It was 1935. Dad is tall, handsome, wearing a double-breasted white suit with a rose in the lapel. The sleeves are a trifle short. My mother stands beside him, holding his arm. Seldom have I seen a face as open, caring and gentle as my mother's. I don't see it immediately as her face. It is so young, childlike almost. But it is her. Her head is tilted slightly to one side, her shoulders to the other. The look on her face is so content and unselfish that my heart aches, but I smile as well.

July 22

I am back in California. Dad is much sicker. He was hospitalized two days ago with acute dehydration. He eats and drinks almost nothing. He has no appetite and has lost ten pounds in the last two weeks, weight he can ill afford to lose. He must be near 140 pounds. IV's are sustaining him now. He has regained strength in the past few days.

My mother sounds tired but strong. She has

recovered from her terrible fall in the Toronto Airport while returning from the Quebec Clinic where Dad went for a special new cancer treatment. My brother, Steve, is flying up to the cottage this weekend. I'm glad. He has seen them very little in the past three years and Dad may die soon. He became quite confused and disoriented before going into the hospital, due to a heightened calcium level in his system, combined with dehydration. The IVs increase the fluids, lowering the calcium concentration, and his mind becomes clearer.

July 25

I called Michigan last night. Dad was just released from the hospital. I wanted to talk to him, to hear his voice, to gauge his condition for myself.

My mother did not recognize my voice when she answered. She half-chuckled in embarrassment, realizing finally that it was me on the phone. We spoke for a moment. Her voice was wan, indistinct. "Your father is very tired," she said. "Very tired."

July 31

Dad regained his lucidity and natural talkativeness after being on the IV's. His calcium level dropped to "high normal." Steve stayed three days, during which Dad talked sometimes for two hours at a stretch—about his finances, college sports, his years of Democratic party politics, but especially about his finances, as he had with me in June. He is intensely proud and independent. As he loses control over his body, as his physical strength and mobility diminish, that he can still care financially for his wife and household becomes increasingly important to him. It is his last connection with his once considerable strength.

<u>August 13</u>

I flew back to Michigan two days ago. Mom called me on Sunday. "Your father has taken a turn for the worse," she said.

My mother is not prone to overstatement or excitability, but I heard the vaguest tremble inside her voice. Thirty minutes later she called back to say she hadn't wanted to alarm me, but simply to let me know how Dad was doing.

"I know, Mom," I said.

I decided right then to fly home the next morning.

I sit watching him across the hospital room. The IV tube is connected to his arm. His mouth is open in a fitful sleep. Now and then his left arm swings up in an arc, as if warding off some threatening spirit, pushing some menace away.

He is remarkably weaker than he was seven weeks ago, when I was last here. I am shocked at the change. He cannot even shift or move his legs in bed. He can barely bring a glass to his lips or form his mouth to speak a word. Even turning on his side in bed to be washed is impossible — he must be rolled over with someone else's strength.

The body breaks down. 200,000 people will die today. 70,000,000 around the world will die this year. 70,000,000 people! Think of it. Yet we spend most — sometimes all — of our lives denying the inevitability of our own fate. Hiding in the cave of fear or denial that keeps many of us from truly living while we are here.

Dad's calcium level has increased again, which affects his thinking and orientation. He gets confused and very paranoid. His bed faces the window so he can see the sky and trees, but he thinks people are outside with rifles waiting to shoot him. He thinks they want to torture him first. He tells my mother and me not to open the shades so they won't be able to get a good shot at him. Sometimes he thinks they're trying to poison his food and we have to taste it first in front of him before he'll eat.

August 19

11:10pm — I am sitting in Dad's room at Munson Hospital in Traverse City. He's endured a particularly hard day. He grows progressively weaker. Fluid builds up in his left lung, causing him to gasp for air amidst a deep gurgling from his chest and throat. He can barely whisper. Mom's greatest fear is that he might die alone, at night, with none of us near him, so we'll keep a 24-hour vigil. I will stay through the night, even though death seems a remote possibility at this point. Still, I am shocked at the change since yesterday. He had seemed better than he'd been in days, even smiling and chuckling a bit.

It is difficult to watch him suffer through this ordeal. They had to "suction" his lungs three times today, inserting a tube through his nostril to suck out the fluid that chokes him. He is so near death. I wish sometimes that there were some plug to pull, some energy to cut off that he might slide more easily into the next phase of his existence.

My brother Mike arrived today from Wisconsin and saw Dad for the first time since May. He didn't recognize him at first. He thought it was another person, so much has he aged in the past few months. Two strong impressions stayed with him: For the first time, Dad looks "like a very old man, like he's ninety"; and the hope that his death would come soon and stop this suffering.

My father is old, yet beautiful as I watch him sleep. His hair is as white as the feathers of a swan. At times, between periods of agitation and movement, he has short spells that seem utterly peaceful and calm. He has not come to terms yet with his impending death. I see the fear in his eyes and the set of his jaw. I want to calm him, to assure him he needn't be so afraid—but he never mentions the subject and I find myself unable to bring it up. A sense of calm about his own dying is a place at which only he can arrive, no matter how much comfort we try to be. Only he can die his death.

I walked along Lake Michigan and watched the sun set at the mouth of the Platte River last night. The sun expanded in size to a huge crimson ball before it descended through a bank of clouds and disappeared. As a child I skipped stones there for hours. The river, washing the pebbles for hundreds of years, has flattened them into perfect, round orbs that skip with a delicate grace across the smooth surface of the water.

Stones have always mesmerized me. I collected them endlessly as a child: from Platte Lake, from the beaches along Lake Michigan, from this same Platte River where they are washed so smooth. On the mantel in my house I have a little "rock garden" of three stones that are special to me: A roughly hewn lapis lazuli elephant, one inch high, that I bought in India for a dollar 25 years ago; a tiny carved jade Fu Dog that Laura gave me on our wedding day; and a patterned "Petosky" stone from this same shore at Lake Michigan. As I sat on the beach watching the sun redden the western sky, I decided to find a stone to remember my father by, a stone from this spot I've loved all my life, to which he first brought me when I was three years old—a stone he would hold in his hand before he died, into which he would pass some part of his spirit and power to live on with me as a symbol of his life and fatherhood.

I began searching along the shoreline for the right stone, one of character and beauty. I found three—one beige, one a deep charcoal gray, the last a patterned dark orange. Tonight, sitting in the parking lot outside the hospital, I made the final choice—the deep gray stone with its smooth and slightly mottled surface.

A few hours ago, during one of Dad's wakeful periods, I placed the stone in his hand.

"Will you hold this for a little while, Dad?" I said. He took it in his hand. "It's a stone from the mouth of the river. Some of your spirit and power will go into it and stay with me."

When I said this, he pushed the stone away as if it were radioactive, with terror in his eyes.

The night hours pass slowly but feel precious to me. Dad sleeps again, sometimes quietly, often agitated. His left hand keeps waving a kind of circle in the air, as if shooing away some demon. I love this man deeply. I realize I will miss him terribly.

August 20

He is much better today. His lungs are clearer and he breathes more easily, though this is relative. He still labors for breath. I don't witness this directly. My brother Mike tells me. He and his wife relieved me at the hospital at 8 am. Mom goes up later.

I am tired. I slept for perhaps an hour last night at the hospital. I stay at the cottage feeling vague all day, trying to rest, thinking, reading in the sun. I mow the lawn and relish the smooth clipped lines of the grass against the glassy surface of the lake. The summer has been wet, in contrast to the southeast where the worst drought in a hundred years is ravaging the land and farmers. Here the lake is as high as I ever remember. The grass is startlingly green.

A kind of completion takes place today. Mike's oldest son, Michael, was here a few months ago, helping out when Dad's arm and leg were broken. Mike brought his other five kids this time, and they all go to the hospital to visit their grandpa. Now all of the seventeen grandchildren, except Steve's daughter Ellen, who is in South America, have seen him in the past few months. Even Tom's kids from California were here. Dad recognizes all five, acknowledges them all even though he can no longer speak. A poignant moment passes between him and Timmy, the youngest grandchild at ten years old. They have a special bond. They fished in Canada and played poker together for hours, the oldest and

Father

youngest of our clan. As Timmy is about to leave the room, grandpa points his finger at him and winks, as if to say, "Go get 'em, Skooter."

Tomorrow we will move Dad by ambulance the 200 miles to my sister's house in southern Michigan. My mother simply cannot handle the strain of caring for him up north here. He is incontinent, hasn't the strength even to turn on his side. The number of days he is allowed in the hospital under the health insurance is nearly over. He would be transferred to a nursing or medical care facility and we all decided that to spend his last days at home with his family would be far better. I had desperately hoped that we could move him back to the cottage for a few days before the transfer south because he loves it so much. His spirit is here. But the doctor said he is too weak, that the extra move would be too much—which means he will never see his beloved Platte Lake again.

Everyone is back from the hospital now for dinner. Dad seems stable, much better than yesterday. The nurses have not suctioned his lungs all day. Last week Mike and Timmy drove to Canada to fish, and tonight we barbecue smallmouth bass from their trip that this morning were frozen in a block of ice.

The plans are set for the ambulance transfer in the morning—the "Transfer Prescription" signed by Dr. Zachman; oxygen and IV monitoring en route; electric hospital bed and two shifts of nursing care at Susan's house. A "No Code" order is signed for the trip, saying that in case Dad stops breathing he is not to be resuscitated by forced or artificial means. But this is a formality—he'll certainly make it through the journey and probably into sometime in September.

    At dinner we discuss the final arrangements for the morning and whether it is necessary for someone to stay with him through the night. The hospital is 40 miles away, we'll be leaving early tomorrow, and he seems stable, noticeably better. But finally we decide that someone should be with him, since this is the last night he will be at the hospital and not at home, the last time he would be alone with strangers. If by some quirk of fate he took a sudden turn and died, Mother would never forgive herself if he were alone. I will drive up after dinner, then Mike's wife, Mary Ann, will come up about 1:00 am, so I can get some rest before closing the cottage and driving south tomorrow.

Halfway to the hospital in Traverse City I see the full moon rise over the eastern forests. It is magnificent—a mammoth sphere of soft light, deep yellow orange, more striking even than the harvest moon in October. I am so struck by this moon that I pull over to the side of the road and get out to watch it. Then I drive until I find a phone booth at a closed gas station and call my mother to tell her to go out and look at this spectacular moon. They have just come back inside from doing that very thing.

    The Tigers baseball game is on the car radio. They are playing the California Angels in Detroit. I listen abstractly, thinking about my father, my family and my childhood. About this place in the woods of Northern Michigan. It is the seventh inning. A few moments after hearing the line score, I think vaguely, "Did he say, 'California, no runs, no hits, no errors?'" No hits? I hadn't been listening so I didn't catch it. But wouldn't that be something? After the break Ernie Harwell, the Tigers' announcer, comes back on. His voice is cranked a notch above normal. I had heard correctly. Walt Terrell is pitching a no-hitter in the eighth inning. The fans are starting to clap continuously. Six more batters to go. Terrell gets through the inning in about 10 pitches—three up, three down. The Tigers hit a home run in the bottom of the eighth for a 3-0 lead, and it's into the ninth. Three more outs to go. The fans are on their feet, yelling, hoping, anticipating this bit of history. The first batter pops out to the third baseman. One down! The Tigers have not pitched a no-hitter in Detroit since 1952. I turn into the hospital parking lot and Ernie Harwell's voice rises with each pitch. Up steps the next batter. He lifts a soft fly to the outfield. Two outs! The fans go crazy, pounding, stomping, cheering Terrell on. A no-hitter is one out away. It is the baseball equivalent of scaling Everest. The first baseman, Wally Joyner, who was the first rookie ever voted to start the All-Star game, walks to the plate. There's a striking coincidence: two months ago he came to bat in the ninth inning of Charlie Hough's no-hit bid for Texas. On that occasion Joyner lined a single to spoil it. Here he is again. The ninth inning. Two outs. He's the only batter between Walt Terrell and inclusion in baseball history. Harwell's voice is off the register. The stadium is pandemonium. Terrell winds. He pitches. Joyner swings at the first pitch and rips the ball into the rightfield corner for a clean double. A stunned silence falls on the stadium. The magic no-hitter is gone, that fast. The next batter makes an out and the game is over. So close. But a one-hitter is like climbing the Appalachians next to the Everest of a no-hitter. I turn off the car and curse Joyner for stealing Terrell's thrill of a lifetime.

Dad is dozing as I enter the room. He seems agitated, fitful, as is often the case. Karen, the nurse, comes in. The nurses have been wonderful. Dad hasn't spent too hard an evening, she says. Quite stable and breathing without terrible difficulty. They just changed him twenty minutes ago.

A short time later he wakes and sees me. I stroke his shoulder, take his hand. He is so frail, so weak, yet he looks so frightened.

"Are you all right, Dad?" I ask. "Are you comfortable?"

He nods.

"Are you in much pain?"

He shakes his head, but I wonder. I have seen him grimace hard when they move him or raise the bed. The cancer is also in his spine.

He tries to speak to me. For three or four minutes he fights to communicate, at first with whispers, then, gathering his strength, with louder bursts from his chest. But I can understand nothing. All that comes out are a few unintelligible noises, broken sounds. It is difficult to watch his frustration. His mind functions, but his body no longer works. He hasn't the strength and finally stops trying. I look hard into his eyes, trying to read his thoughts. But I can't.

I tell him about the baseball game and Walt Terrell's near no-hitter. He loves baseball and loves the Tigers. He

Father

played semi-pro ball himself, and might have gone further but for his torn-up knee. But he doesn't seem to hear me, or care about what I'm saying. His eyes are wide open, but they look confused, afraid. For weeks I have wanted to speak to him about death, to find out what's going on in his mind, but have not been able to mention it. Suddenly, I feel I must.

"Do you believe in an afterlife, Dad?" I ask.

Quickly, his eyes look away from me, to the left, then upward, then left again. He doesn't try to speak, but grabs the railing of the bed with his left hand.

"Do you believe in an afterlife?" I ask him again gently.

As I say the words he looks at me, then looks away again quickly, looking frightened, trapped.

"You don't have to be afraid, Dad. You don't have to be afraid. You're going to a place much better than here. Your body is not your spirit, it is not you. You, all of us, will go to a place that's safe, that's warm and peaceful and very loving. All of us will die. I may die before you do. And we'll all go to this better, safer place. Our spirit, our true life, goes on from here."

All the while that I speak he looks at me, into my eyes.

"I want to read you something," I say. I have read to him several times over the past days. He loves reading. I reach into my bag for a book and hold it up before him.

"This book is called 'Life After Life'. It is written by a doctor. Dr. Raymond Moody. He researched and studied over 150 people who died, clinically, then were brought back to life through the incredible medical, technical means we have available today. They were actually dead. And through his research he found that they all go through a very similar experience. It's somewhat different for different people, but this is a fundamental description of what it's like."

I begin to read.

"'A man is dying, and as he reaches the point of greatest physical distress, he hears himself pronounced dead by his doctor. He begins to hear an uncomfortable noise, a loud ringing or buzzing, and at the same time feels himself moving very rapidly through a long dark tunnel. After this, he suddenly finds himself outside his own physical body, but still in the immediate physical environment, and he sees his own body from a distance, as though he is a spectator. He watches the resuscitation attempt from this unusual vantage point and is in a state of emotional upheaval.

"'After awhile, he collects himself and becomes more accustomed to his odd condition. He notices that he still has a "body," but one of a very different nature and with very different powers from the physical body he has just left behind. Some other things begin to happen. Others come to meet and to help him. He glimpses the spirits of relatives and friends who have already died, and a loving, warm spirit of a kind he has never encountered before—a being of light—appears before him. This being asks him a question, nonverbally, to make him evaluate his life and help him along by showing him a panoramic, instantaneous playback of the major events of his life. At some point he finds himself approaching some sort of barrier or border, apparently representing the limit between earthly life and the next life.... He is overwhelmed by intense feelings of joy, love, and peace. And usually, when these beings are resuscitated or brought back to life, they are so taken with their experiences in the afterlife that they don't want to return.'

"You don't have to worry, Dad. You don't have to be afraid."

During the time I read and speak, his countenance changes dramatically. He is still aware and awake. His eyes are open. But he seems peaceful. His face is totally different now, the muscles relaxed instead of tense. He looks up at me and I am almost startled by the calm in his eyes, which before had been so tormented and afraid.

"There are a few more things I want to read to you," I say, "about these people who were brought back to life and how they felt after their experience of dying.

"One says, 'After I came back, I cried off and on for about a week because I had to live in this world after seeing that one. I didn't want to come back.'

"Another says, 'When I came back, I brought with me some of the wonderful feelings I had over there. They lasted for several days. Even now I feel them sometimes.'

"And a third says, 'This feeling was so indescribable. It has stayed with me in a way. I've never forgotten it.'"

Dad gazes off to the left, a pensive, quiet look on his face. He looks at me, and again I am startled by the peacefulness and calm in him. He looks to the left and then we are quiet, together there on his bed.

A few minutes later he sucks in a breath and it stays within him so long that I become alarmed. Finally he breathes out and in again hard. This time the breath holds within him even longer, what seems like two or three minutes. I almost call the nurse, but decide to just stay here with him. He is perfectly still, calm, silent. And I think, tears in my eyes, unbelieving, that my father is dead in front of me, his eyes open. Suddenly, loud enough to make me jump, his body convulses and gasps in another great breath. He grips the bed railing with his left hand. He grimaces hard for a few seconds. Then his body relaxes...and he dies. I know that he is dead this time, and that he found peace before he went.

I lay my head on his chest, holding him, feeling his warmth against my face. Tears fill my eyes and I feel humbled, privileged, to have shared this parting, sorry that my mother is not here.

I stay there for several minutes, crying, holding him. But it is a quiet crying, one of loss and passing but not of pain. I know he is all right. I feel his spirit surrounding me in the room.

"Thank you, Dad, for all your love, your sacrifices, your protection. For all you have given us. We love you very, very much."

I look at his face. It has the peace of a bird gliding in soft flight, the peace of Platte Lake at sunset.

After a while I leave his bedside and call my mother. When she gets on the phone I can't speak for a moment.

"Mom, I have something to tell you.... Dad died a few minutes ago."

I hear her breath stop. For months she has prepared herself for this, but still she isn't ready. Probably we never are. The words shock her. He'd been so much better today. Everything was set for the move downstate in the morning. Now he's dead?

I hear her crying. We lead our minds through the anticipation of loss, like astronauts preparing for space, but we can never know the sensations and emotions until the day arrives. Fifty-two years they were married. She was nineteen when they met, now she is seventy-three. How does one anticipate such change?

We talk for a few minutes on the phone. She and Mike and Mary Ann, Mike's wife, will drive up to the hospital right away. I hang up and go back into Dad's room. His body is utterly still and peaceful. After a while I touch his hand and feel that it has cooled. This startles me. I realize with my senses that he is dead. The fire is out inside him. What changes? I wonder. What is this force that allows us to be alive? His body is still here, intact, all the blood, the nerves, the muscles. But now it is just matter, already turning cold. What gives it energy and animation? What causes the life in it? Scientists can assemble all the components of a living organism in the laboratory. They can replicate the precise temperature and biochemistry. But they cannot create life. What is this force? Where does it come from? How does it work? Is it spirit? Soul? Is it God inside us, inside all living things?

Mom arrives with Mike and Mary Ann. Her steps are both hurried and halting. She is anxious to reach the room, but afraid of what she must encounter there. I hug her. She cries on my chest. She looks into my eyes, then the four of us go over to Dad's bed. Her hand reaches out to touch his hand. I can see in her the tremendous love she feels for him, and the loss, and a sense of relief that his terrible suffering is over.

After a few minutes Mike, Mary Ann and I leave her alone with him, to say goodbye to this man, now dead, that she has shared her life with for more than fifty years.

Photographs

PAGE 26   Family Holiday Photo

PAGE 29   Kids in Boat with Dad

PAGE 41   Susan and Her Five Brothers

PAGE 43   Susan and Young Peter

PAGE 47   Mom with Baby Mike and Brother Johnny

PAGE 52   Mom and Grampa with the Six Kids

PAGE 70   Peter and Mom in the Backyard at Cottage

PAGE 85   Peter and Steve with a Big Catch

PAGE 121 Family with the Car

PAGE 140 Bess and John

PAGE 145 Peter in the Peruvian Andes

PAGE 172 Grampa and Dad

PAGE 202 John and Bess on Their Wedding Day

Acknowledgements

This book formed over time and through journeys both literal and internal. My heartfelt thanks to friends too numerous to mention who contributed directly, indirectly, and in ways in which they are likely unaware.

I particularly wish to thank Suzanne Anderson-Carey —who created all the illustrations featured here—for her always brilliant artistic and design talents. Marian O'Brien and Keith Whitaker of O'Brien & Whitaker Publishers, without whose support, expertise, inspiration and hard work this book would not exist. And my family— Bess and John, my sister Susan, and my four brothers, all of whom helped form the core of who I am.

And special thanks to Meoy, Santi and Isabelle.

Berkeley, California
December 2018

ABOUT THE AUTHOR

Peter Damm's life has traveled varied tracks. He was raised in small town rural Michigan and graduated with Honors from the University of Michigan in Ann Arbor. He later studied with National Book Award winner Wright Morris, and with Guggenheim Fellow and National Jewish Book Award winner Leo Litwak in the Master's Creative Writing Program at San Francisco State University. He has lived abroad and traveled widely in Europe, India, Bali, Mexico, and parts of the Middle East, Indonesia, Central and South America, and New Zealand. He worked on the grounds crew of a golf course, as a banquet waiter, on road construction crews, the staffs of magazines, and as a freelance writer and editor. He has taught European travel classes, taught English language and American culture to Japanese university students, co-founded an import gourmet food business, was co-owner of a residential real estate brokerage, earned a doctorate degree in Clinical Psychology at the Wright Institute in Berkeley, and worked as a psychotherapist, grief counselor, and with families of the chronically mentally ill. His book of poems, *At the Water's Edge*, chronicles a 5-month journey in Bali, Indonesia and New Zealand. Peter lives and works in Berkeley, California.